The Gospel (?) of Destruction

"And this gospel of the kingdom will be preached in all the world as a witness to all the nations, and then the end will come."

How Could Jesus Call the Message of the Impending Fall of Jerusalem, the Gospel (the "Good News!") of the Kingdom?

ISBN - 9781706703013

Logo Design: Joseph Vincent

Cover Design by:
Jeffrey T. McCormack
The Pendragon: Web and Graphic Design
www.the pendragon.net

A preliminary word:

For years I have pondered why, in the Biblical texts, the destruction of Jerusalem was clearly so important. I have wondered why that event was so heavily emphasized in many of the early writings and used as an effective proof of Christ's Deity, and yet, once past the fourth century, the importance of that horrific event seems to have all but faded from the polemic and apologetic mind–set of the church. In today's modern church, there is virtually no recognition of the importance of the fall of Jerusalem.

As I will share in this book, numerous debate opponents have literally scoffed at the fall of Jerusalem as if it were a totally insignificant event, having no spiritual meaning whatsoever; "Who cared if Jerusalem was destroyed?" It has been exclaimed. This is, lamentably, far too common.

I hope that after reading this work the reader will begin to grasp what a horrific, yet necessary and wonderful, yes, *wonderful*, the taking away of that symbol of the Old Covenant world truly was—even for us today. It was clearly not "wonderful" due to the horrific loss of human life that took place, no, but, it was and is "good news" because of what it heralded—the full arrival of the New Covenant World of Jesus, wherein righteousness, life and eternal fellowship with our God dwells. I hope you will give this book careful consideration so that you can better understand what I mean by "the Gospel of Destruction."

My special thanks to my friend Scott Fisher for generating the scripture and topical indices. My thanks to all the readers of the Kindle version of this book who have encouraged me to put this in paperback.

Don K. Preston D. Div.
Preterist Research Institute
www.donkpreston.com
www.bibleprophecy.com

Table of Contents

Point # 1 – Page 1f—The Gospel of Destruction?
How Could Jesus Call the Message of the Impending Fall of
Jerusalem, the Gospel (the "Good News!") of the Kingdom?

Point # 2 – Page 16f—It Was the Time of The Glorification
of the Saints

Point # 3 – Page 20f—The Removal of the Old Covenant
World Was The Full Bloom of the New Creation

Point # 4 – Page 28f—The Time of the Fall of Jerusalem
Was The Time of the Regathering/Restoration of Israel
(Mt. 24:31).

Point # 5 – Page 45f—It Was the Time of the Fulfillment of
Key Old Testament Eschatological Prophecies

Point # 6 – Page 51f—The Fall of Jerusalem Was the Time
of the Fulfillment of All Things—Answering Some
Objections

Point # 7 – Page 84f—The Fall of Jerusalem was The End
of the Age of Shadows and Types—The Reality Came!

Point # 8 – Page 93f—It Was When Man Could Enter the
Most Holy Place and Receive Salvation!—The End of the
Ministration of Death.

Point # 9 – Page 103f—It was the Consummation of the
Eschatological Wrath of God—It Was the Time of
Redemption!

Point # 10 – Page 113f—The Fall of Jerusalem—the Capital of the Old Kingdom, Meant the Full Arrival of the New Covenant Kingdom!

Point # 11 – Page 120f—Because the End of the Old Covenant Age Was the Time of the Resurrection and New Creation

Point #12 – Page 144f—Special Study—<u>Not Found in the Kindle Version</u>—A Look at Matthew 8:11: Jesus, Abraham, the Resurrection and AD 70.

Point # 13 – Page 164f—Special Study—<u>Not Found in the Kindle Version</u> The Destruction of the Temple and Cultus Powerfully and Effectively Put an End to the Judaizing Movement

Point # 14 – Page 174f—Restoring "the Gospel of Destruction."

Index of Scriptures – Page 189f

Topical Index – Page 193f

The Gospel of Destruction

"And this gospel of the kingdom will be preached in all the world as a witness to all the nations, and then the end will come."

Point # 1–Preliminary Discussion

How Could Jesus Call the Message of the Impending Fall of Jerusalem, the Gospel (the "Good News!") of the Kingdom?

Jesus' words in Matthew 24:14, in what is known as the Olivet Discourse, have been and continue to be the cause of a tremendous amount of eschatological speculation.

Jesus had just been asked by his disciples for the sign of his parousia (his presence) and the end of the age (24:3). Verse 14 is part of his direct answer. Modern evangelicals claim constantly that the Gospel has never been preached into all the world until modern times, when as a result of the Internet and social media, we now have for the first time in history the ability to preach the Gospel into all the world. But, that suggestion overlooks or ignores several factors:

1. Jesus was not speaking of the global "world" when he said the Gospel would be preached into all the world.

2. The NT writers are very clear, stating it emphatically, that the Gospel had been preached into all the world, in their generation.

3. Very often, following directly on their assertions that the Gospel had been preached into all the world, they then said that the end,

Christ's coming, was near, at hand and coming soon.[1]

It is critical to see that in Matthew 24:14 when Jesus foretold the preaching of the Gospel into all the world prior to the fall of Jerusalem that he was not simply predicting the preaching of the gospel (generically considered) into all the world. Unfortunately, that is how this text is normally considered. But that is not what he said. He literally said that "*this **the** gospel* of the kingdom must be preached into all the world." The Greek is τοῦτος *(this)* τό *(the)* εὐαγγέλιον (Gospel or good news). He was speaking of a very specific "good news."

What was "*this the gospel*" he was referring to? The antecedent discussion shows that it was the message of the impending end of the Old Covenant Age and the fall of Jerusalem. Jesus was not referring to the Gospel comprehensively considered or defined. It was a very specifically defined bit of "good news" that he was referring to.

That is not to say that the Gospel comprehensively defined was not *included*, because the proclamation of the Gospel of Christ, crucified, buried and resurrected, meant that the New Creation had broken in. That signaled the "beginning of the end" of the Old. Thus, my comments should not, in any sense be construed as saying that the Gospel comprehensively defined was not to be—and was not—preached into the world. My main focus is the immediate context of Matthew 24 that shows that the "good news," *the very specific good news* that Jesus had in mind in Matthew 24:14, was the declaration and prediction of the end of the Old Covenant age. This is important

---

[1] For a demonstration of this, see my book, *Into All The World, Then Comes The End*. In that book, I show, with an abundance of evidence, that the NT testimony is clear, unequivocal and explicit in affirming that the Gospel had been preached into all the world. My book is available on my websites, Amazon, Kindle, and other retailers.

for understanding Jesus' comments in Matthew 24:14. With this in mind, we will proceed.

Those who accept the Biblical testimony that Christ came in the first century, (what is known as preterism) at the end of the Old Covenant age are often accused of not preaching the Gospel. We are told that we ride a hobby horse. We are accused of preaching a gospel that has no hope.

Sam Frost, former preterist, stated on Facebook, in one of his many diatribes against Covenant Eschatology, that nothing could be worse than believing a system or doctrine that has no hope—an on–going, unfulfilled hope of the supposed end of time. Preterists say that all promises and prophecies are fulfilled, thus, preterists are preaching a "hopeless" gospel, and that is *horrible*, says Mr. Frost. Based on this "logic," if it can be called that, when all prophecy is finally fulfilled, and there is no longer any "hope" Christians will be living in a horrible world—the world of fulfillment. How terrible! Mr. Frost is purposefully ignoring Proverbs 13:12, (He knows the text well)— "Hope deferred makes the heart sick. A promise fulfilled is a tree of life." But evidently, Mr. Frost prefers "hope" to the tree of life.

Millennial author Joel Richardson stated in a Twitter discussion— "Full preterism fails to meet the basic criteria of actually being 'good news.'" (Twitter feed 5-15-18).

In that Twitter exchange, when I invited Mr. Richardson to engage me in formal debate, his response was to accuse me of arrogance, condescension, and dishonesty. He then accused me and other preterists of denying that Christ "is human in any way." When I asked him to prove his (slanderous) claim by citing any preterist who believes that, he blocked me from his Twitter feed. He subsequently blocked other preterists for asking for documentation of his claims.

For those interested, I produced a YouTube series reviewing and responding to Mr. Richardson's book, *Mystery Babylon: Unraveling the Bible's Greatest Mystery*. You can find those videos by going to YouTube and searching for my name and my series "Responding to Mr. Richardson." Mr. Richardson's book is rife with theological error, exegetical failings, anachronistic assumptions, and logical fallacies. It utterly fails to convince.

Similarly, Brock Hollett, another former preterist attempting to falsify preterism published a book denying any redemptive meaning to the fall of Jerusalem.[2] I have produced a YouTube video series reviewing his book and refuting his claims. You can view that series of videos on my YouTube channel by doing a search.

The question is proper to ask, does full preterism fail to meet the basic criteria of actually being "good news"? The question can also be asked: Is it better to have hope than to have the fulfillment of hope?

Let's allow the Bible—and Jesus himself—to answer these questions, by looking at Matthew 23–24.

In chapter 23:37, Jesus, standing in the temple, had pronounced coming judgment on that holy place: "Your house is left to you desolate." This is the context for the beginning of chapter 24 where the disciples begin to show Jesus the stones of the temple. The beauty of that temple must have been astounding!

As Jesus and his disciples left that grand edifice and went east across the Kidron valley to the Mount of Olives, Jesus told the disciples that the time was coming when the temple would be utterly destroyed. In response, the disciples began to ask, "Tell us, when shall these things be, and what shall be the sign of your coming and the end of the age."

---

[2] Brock Hollett, *Debunking Preterismn*, (Kearney, NE; Morris Publishing, 2018).

4

It is commonly believed, in fact, the majority opinion among commentators is that the disciples were confused and wrongly believed that the temple would not—indeed, could not—be destroyed until the so–called "end of time." John Calvin went so far as to say that the disciples, "did not suppose that while the building of this world stood, the temple could fall to ruins." The disciples were therefore mistaken in their questions.[3]

The fact is, it was not the ancient disciples of Jesus that were confused, but rather the modern commentators. It is far easier to ascribe ignorance and confusion to the ancient disciples than it is to admit that perhaps the modern commentators are wrong! I cannot discuss this issue extensively here, but, see my book, *We Shall Meet Him In The Air, the Wedding of the King of kings.*[4] In that book, I show conclusively that the disciples were not confused. They did not even believe in any such thing as "the end of time." Not only that, they well understood, from their own prophecies, that the end of the age coming of the Lord was to be at the time of the destruction of Israel and her power. And finally, when Jesus asked them if they understood those OT prophecies of the end of the age, they answered unambiguously, "Yes."

Turning back to the text of Matthew 24, Jesus began to answer the disciples' questions about the signs of the end of the age. Notice particularly Matthew 24:14:

"This gospel of the kingdom shall be preached into all the world, for

---

[3] John Calvin, *Calvin's Commentaries*, (Grand Rapids; Baker, XVII, 2005), 117.

[4] Don K. Preston, *We Shall Meet Him In The Air, the Wedding of the King of kings,* (Ardmore, Ok; JaDon Management Inc. 2010). The book is available on my websites, Amazon, Kindle and other retailers.

a witness to the nations, then comes the end."

Jesus was answering the disciples' questions about the signs of the end of the age. He said that one of the signs of the end would be the fulfillment of the World Mission. But, did you notice what he called that? Once again, he said, "*This* gospel (good news) of the kingdom shall be preached." What "*this* gospel of the kingdom" was he referencing? He was speaking of the proclamation of the coming fall of Jerusalem! And he called that message of the coming destruction "*this* gospel of the *kingdom*."

How in the name of reason could Jesus call that horrific catastrophe the "good news" i.e. the gospel, and then, how could he call it "this gospel, this *good news*, of the *kingdom*"? How is the destruction of the Old Covenant City, Temple, and people good news and how was it related to the *kingdom*? There are many reasons why that event was "good news," but lamentably, these reasons are commonly overlooked (or ignored) by all but a few commentators through the ages. So, how could Jesus call that message of coming disaster "good news"? There are numerous reasons, and I will cover only a few of them.

＊It was good news for Jesus' followers because the destruction of Jerusalem would mean relief from the organized persecution of the church by the Jewish authorities.

In chapter 23 Jesus spoke of the coming persecution as he spoke to those who would be guilty of the internecine policy:

> Therefore you are witnesses against yourselves that you are sons of those who murdered the prophets. Fill up, then, the measure of your fathers' guilt. Serpents, brood of vipers! How can you escape the condemnation of hell? Therefore, indeed, I send you prophets, wise men, and scribes: some of them you will kill and crucify, and some of them you will

scourge in your synagogues and persecute from city to city, that on you may come all the righteous blood shed on the earth, from the blood of righteous Abel to the blood of Zechariah, son of Berechiah, whom you murdered between the temple and the altar. Assuredly, I say to you, all these things will come upon this generation (Matthew 23:31–36).

So, Jerusalem would be the epicenter and the source of the organized persecution of Christ's followers—"it is not possible that a prophet perish outside of Jerusalem" (Luke 13:33).

Justin the Martyr, second century, wrote in his polemic against the Jew, Trypho:

For other nations have not inflicted on us and on Christ this wrong to such an extent as you have, who in very deed are the authors of the wicked prejudice against the Just One, and us who hold by Him. For after that you had crucified Him, the only blameless and righteous Man,—through whose stripes those who approach the Father by Him are healed,—when you knew that He had risen from the dead and ascended to heaven, as the prophets foretold He would, you not only did not repent of the wickedness which you had committed, but at that time you selected and sent out from Jerusalem chosen men through all the land to tell that the godless heresy of the Christians had sprung up, and to publish those things which all they who knew us not speak against us. So that you are the cause not only of your own unrighteousness, but in fact of that of all other men. (*Against Trypho*, Chapter XVII).

Notice that what Justin accused the Jews of doing is precisely what

Jesus foretold:

> At that time you selected and sent out from Jerusalem
> chosen men through all the land to tell that the
> godless heresy of the Christians had sprung up, and to
> publish those things which all they who knew us not
> speak against us. So that you are the cause not only of
> your own unrighteousness, but in fact of that of all
> other men.

Justin is clearly referring to Jesus' generation and the actions of the
Jewish leaders of that time, because Jerusalem had been destroyed by
the time he wrote.

Adolph Harnack stated:

> Unless the evidence is misleading, they instigated the
> Neronic outburst against Christians; and as a rule,
> whenever bloody persecutions were afoot in later
> days, the Jews are either in the background or the
> foreground.[5]

N. T. Wright observes:

> Persecution of Christians did not in fact, initially
> come from pagans. He continues, In fact, the
> earliest and best evidence we possess for serious and
> open hostility between Jews—especially
> Pharisees—and the nascent Christian movement is
> found in the earliest period for which we have
> evidence, namely in the letters of Paul. He, by his

---

[5] Adolph Harnack, *Mission and Expansion of
Christianity,* Harper and Brothers, 1961), 57+.

own admission, had persecuted the very early church with violence and zeal.[6]

Thus, when Jesus, in Matthew 23–24, predicted the coming destruction of Jerusalem, he was essentially predicting the end of the organized, centralized Jewish persecution of the church. We find this promise throughout the NT epistles, the coming judgment of the persecutors of the early church. This is found in Romans, in Galatians, in Thessalonians, in Hebrews, in James, in Peter, and in Revelation! This is a *dominant* theme and motif in the NT!

As we continue, I will share some of the attendant, additional elements of "good news" that would accompany that prediction of Israel's impending judgment. For now, it is enough to realize that when Jesus predicted the coming destruction of Jerusalem, to his disciples who would be chased "from city to city" by those sent out by the leaders of Jerusalem to kill them, that truly would have been "good news." How could it be anything else?

For more on this issue of martyr vindication, get a copy of my book, *The Resurrection of Daniel 12:2: Fulfilled or Future?*[7] In this tome I demonstrate with abundant evidence, both scriptural and historical, that the Jewish persecution of the first–century saints is a key eschatological tenet and inextricably bound up with the Day of the Lord and the resurrection. For now, let's continue our investigation.

Jesus said that the proclamation of the coming destruction of

---

[6] N. T. Wright, *Jesus and the Victory of God,* (Grand Rapids; Eerdmans, *1996),* 374.

[7] Don K. Preston, *The Resurrection of Daniel 12:2: Fulfilled or Future?,* (Ardmore, Ok; JaDon Management Inc.2016). The book is available on Amazon, Kindle, my websites and other retailers.

Jerusalem was to be preached into all the world, as a witness to the nations, then comes the end. And, as we noted above, he called that coming judgment "this gospel of the kingdom." How in the world could Jesus call the fall of Jerusalem "this gospel" this "good news"?

Jesus would go ahead to describe the coming period as the greatest tribulation ever:

"For then there will be great tribulation, such as has not been since the beginning of the world until this time, no, nor ever shall be." Matthew 24:21

Dispensationalists appeal to this text to deny that Jesus was talking about the Jewish War. They point to WWII and the Holocaust, pointing out that in WWII over 30 million people perished. They ask, wasn't that worse than the Jewish War? Well, they fail to see why Jesus could call the destruction of Jerusalem and the temple as the greatest tribulation ever.

Kenneth Gentry correctly assesses the meaning of Jesus' words:

> In regard to Matthew 24:21 and the great tribulation, Gentry says, "I would argue: first, the covenantal significance of the loss of the temple stands as the most dramatic redemptive–historical outcome of the Jewish War."[8]

In the events of AD 70, the Old Covenant world of Israel came to an end. The Lord's exclusive covenant relationship with Israel (Amos 3:3f) was terminated. Nothing like this had ever happened; *nothing like this will ever happen again*! The New Covenant world of Christ

---

[8] Kenneth Gentry, *He Shall Have Dominion*, (Draper, VA; Apologetics Group, 2009), 347.

that came into full bloom with the dissolution of the Old is eternal. It has no end!

The reality is that the Jewish War was a "good news/bad news" reality. For the New World to come in, the Old World had to pass away. This is why through scripture, when describing the Day of the Lord, the writers speak of it on the one hand as a Day to be dreaded (Amos 5:18f) and yet, it would be the Day of Salvation! See my book, *Elijah Has Already Come: A Solution to Romans 11:25–27* for a full discussion of this. It is fascinating is that so many commentators fail to see that both salvation and judgment come at the same time.

For instance, Kenneth Gentry quoted Thomas Ice in their formal written debate on the Great Tribulation. Ice said:

> A key factor in favor of futurism and literal interpretation is that even if one takes the symbolical approach to the text, the fact that Israel is rescued–not judged–in the Olivet Discourse (except Luke 21:20–24) is unavoidable and thus, a fatal blow to preterism.[9]

Ice clearly believes that it is an either/or situation but, this is patently false. The Day of the Lord was to be, for the righteous, vindication and salvation. It was to be, for the wicked, the time of destruction—see Matthew 25:31f. To be honest, it is somewhat astounding that so many commentators hold to an "either/or" concept. But, back to the idea that the destruction of Jerusalem was to be "good news." What was there, in addition to being the time of the destruction of the persecuting power, that was "good news"?

---

[9] *The Great Tribulation Debate,* Kenneth L. Gentry and Thomas Ice, *The Great Tribulation Past or Future?*, (Grand Rapids, MI; Kregel Publications, 1999), 192.

The "good news" was that the nascent body of Christ would be identified as the true people of God.

In the first century, one of the burning, *key* issues became: Who are the true children of God? Who are the true descendants of Abraham?

Jesus had identified his followers as his "brothers and sisters"—his true family (Matthew 12:49–50). That meant that "family" was no longer by bloodline and race, but through obedience. This was shattering!

In Acts 3:22f, Peter, standing in front of that hostile audience of Jews, had this to say about the necessity of acceptance and obedience to Jesus as the Savior:

> For Moses truly said to the fathers, 'The Lord your God will raise up for you a Prophet like me from your brethren. Him you shall hear in all things, whatever He says to you. And it shall be that every soul who will not hear that Prophet shall be utterly destroyed from among the people.

What was Peter doing? He was identifying the True Israel—the true "*the people*" as those who accepted Jesus! But notice that he warned his audience that those who refused to accept Jesus: "And it shall be that every soul who will not hear that Prophet shall be utterly destroyed from among the people." The language here is graphic— "utter destruction" awaited those who rejected Jesus as Messiah.

Those rejecting Jesus would be "utterly destroyed"—which of course happened in AD 70—but, on the other side of the coin, it meant that with the destruction of the Old People, the True People of God were revealed. The 'sons of God were manifested' just as Paul predicted in Romans 8:19: "For the earnest expectation of the creation eagerly waits for the revealing of the sons of God."

What was "creation" longing for? It was waiting for "the manifestation *(apocalypsis*–the revealing) of the sons of God." In the mind–set of the ancient world, nothing could have more clearly manifested the identity of the True Israel than the destruction of the very symbol of the Old World, the City, and the Temple.

That manifestation of the true sons of God is discussed in 2 Thessalonians 1, a passage that is grossly misapplied to the future.

The church at Thessalonica was being persecuted by the "synagogue of Satan" (Acts 17). But, Paul promised that suffering church that their persecutors would soon have the tables turned on them, "it is a righteous thing with God to repay with tribulation, those who are troubling you, and to give to you who are being troubled, rest, when the Lord Jesus is revealed from heaven" (2 Thessalonians 1:6f). The persecuted would be punished with "everlasting destruction from the presence of the Lord." Those once in the Presence of the Lord would be cast out! That can only refer to Old Covenant Israel–and no one else.

And, what would be a subsequent and consequent "result" of that coming against the persecutors, other than their judgment? It would be the glorification of Jesus, the vindication of the saints, and thus, the manifestation of the church as the True People of God (see verse 10).

Revelation carries this theme also. Jesus commended the church at Philadelphia for their faithfulness. He said, "Indeed I will make those of the synagogue of Satan, who say they are Jews and are not, but lie—indeed I will make them come and worship before your feet, and to know that I have loved you." Revelation 3:9

Here is the manifestation of the sons of God! Here is the vindication of the saints!

David Chilton noted the irony of Revelation 3: "Those who falsely claim to be Jews are really in the position of the persecuting heathen; (he takes note of Jesus' citation of Isaiah 60, DKP) and they will be forced to acknowledge the covenantal status of the Church as the inheritor of the promises to Abraham and Moses. The Church is the true Israel."[10]

And so, throughout the NT we find the promise of the coming vindication of the saints as the True Israel, the True People of God. And that "identification" was to be revealed in the judgment of the persecuting power of the Old People. In covenantal terms, nothing could be more devastating, more revealing, more graphic, and nothing more confirmatory than the destruction of Jerusalem.

For 40 years the early church stated that they were the True Israel because the Messiah had come, and they had accepted him. They were persecuted for that faith, because the historical people of God, Israel by blood, refused to believe that an accursed "man of Galilee" was their anticipated Messiah. But, their brethren repeatedly told them, they preached the message into all the world, that the Old Way was coming to an end. They pointed to Jesus' prediction in the Olivet Discourse. And when that predicted destruction was so dramatically, undeniably fulfilled, the church was vindicated, glorified, manifested as the "sons of God."

The early church pointed to the fulfillment of Jesus' prediction repeatedly in their polemics against the Jews and in their evangelistic work among the pagans. And that message was *incredibly effective*. So much so that Julian the Apostate, fourth–century Roman emperor, who had been raised as a Christian, realizing the evangelistic effectiveness of the fulfillment of Jesus' prophecy, determined to rebuild the temple. He believed that by rebuilding the temple that it would strip the church

---

[10] David Chilton, *Days of Vengeance*, (Ft. Worth; Dominion Press, 1987), 128.

14

of one of her most powerful evidences for proving the identity of Jesus. But, his efforts, in spite of the fact that he had the wealth and power of the Roman empire behind him, failed.[11]

One of the great tragedies of the modern Christian church is that it has lost, sometimes on purpose, but, mostly through neglect, the power of the message of "this good news of the kingdom." The end of the Old Covenant age, with the destruction of Jerusalem and the Temple, has been relegated to "local and insignificant" status. After all, as several public debate opponents that I have engaged have said to me, "Why would anyone in Thessalonica, or Athens, or Corinth care about the destruction of a trouble–making Jewish city?" Well, as I have countered: Why would those same people possibly be interested in the crucifixion of just another Jewish rabble–rousing, condemned by both Jewish and Roman courts? The thunderous and absolute silence I have received in "response" to this has been more than revealing.

I suggest that it is high time—and past—to recover the power of the gospel of the kingdom—the "good news" of the end of the Old Covenant world. That event was the manifestation of the sons of God, and irrefutable, undeniable vindication of Jesus as the Son of God. Jesus himself pointed to that event as the sign of his presence—the sign that he is King of kings and Lord of lords (Matthew 24:30). It is time that the modern church begins once again to proclaim that message of victory, of vindication, of identification, of glorification. That truly is good news as we are about to see!

---

[11] See Edward Gibbon, *The Decline and Fall of Roman Empire*, (New York; Random House, Vol. I), 774f.

How Could Jesus Call the Message of the Impending Fall of Jerusalem, the Gospel (the "Good News!") of the Kingdom?

Point # 2

It Was the Time of The Glorification of the Saints

One of the undeniable "good news" aspects of the fall of Jerusalem, that is, good news for the saints then—and now—was—and is—vindication and the subsequent and consequent glorification.

To better understand this claim and this concept, we have to get inside the mind of the ancient Hebrews. If we do not have such insights, much of the message of New Testament eschatology will simply be missed by us. When we come to comprehend the first–century society in which the Bible was written and how powerful the Shame–V–Glory concept was, many of the NT eschatological passages become very clear, and, it becomes glaringly obvious that those passages do not fit any "end of time" scenario.

With this in mind, we need to share, ever so briefly, a few thoughts on this "shame–v–glory" motif as the scholars explain it for us.

Peter Davids and Douglas Moo, discuss the honor–shame motif in the NT times.

> North American society appears guilt motivated (internal feelings predominate), the society of the early church period was honor–shame motivated (external valuations were most important). The surrounding society used shame as a major weapon of persecution (and especially in the cross, where the shaming was as significant as the execution), and the New Testament writers argued for a reversal of

values, showing that Christ and the Christians were in fact the more honorable. They show that the sense of honor and shame is found throughout the NT. In 1 Peter the readers are being shamed by their neighbors (words like 'abuse,' 'insult,' and 'slander' are used), but, it is these neighbors who will receive shame at the final judgment (1 Peter 3:16). The reader's faith, however, will bring them honor when Christ returns (1:7), not shame (2:6). It is they who have the honorable titles given to them.[12]

Likewise, Jerome Neyrey, has a discussion of the honor–shame motif.

Honor is either ascribed to individuals, or achieved by them. Ascribed honor is like inherited wealth: one has it by birth or adoption from a person with the power and status to bestow. Primarily, honor derives from one's clan, family, and father. Sons have the same social status as their father, whether senators or fisherman or artisans ('all should honor the son as they honor the Father' (John 5:23). Honor accrues to one's family name, and all family members share in it when it is publicly acknowledged and respected.

He says (p. 5) that the honor–shame motif "game" contains four elements:
1. Claim to honor
2. Challenge to that claim.
3. Riposte to that Challenge.
4. Public Verdict.

---

[12] Peter H. Davids and Douglas Moo, *1 & 2 Peter* (Grand Rapids; Zondervan, 2002), 27.

He examines Luke 13:10–17 as a "classic example of this challenge–riposte contest" from the life of Jesus that powerfully illustrates the shame–v–honor mentality and the four elements just listed.

He adds: "Ascribed honor, especially that which comes with blood and family, is a group matter; when one member is honored, all are honored; but, when one is shamed, the group shares that loss."[13]

So, honor or shame was something that both the individual and groups shared in, either positively or negatively.

N. T. Wright touches on this motif when he says:

> The whole of the story, of judgment for those who had not followed Jesus and the vindication for those who had, is summed up in the cryptic but frequently repeated saying "the first shall be last, the last first." In other words, when the great tribulation came on Israel, those who had followed Jesus would be delivered; and that would be the sign that Jesus had been in the right, and that in consequence, they had been in the right in following him. The destruction of Jerusalem on the one hand, and the rescue of the disciples on the other, would be the vindication of what Jesus had been saying throughout his ministry.[14]

---

[13] Jerome Neyrey, *2 Peter and Jude*, (New York; DoubleDay; Anchor Bible, 2004), 3f.

[14] N. T. Wright, *Jesus and the Victory of God*, Minneapolis, Fortress, 1996), 338. For more on the shame-v-honor motif and several Biblical examples of this at work, see Randolph Richards, and Brandon J. O' Brien, *Misreading Scripture With Western Eyes,* (Downers Grove; IVP Press, 2012), 113f).

Keep in mind that above we spoke of how the fall of Jerusalem would bring *relief* from the organized Jewish persecution. But, in destroying the Jewish persecutors, the Lord likewise vindicated his saints, and in that event, *he was himself glorified* (Matthew 24:30–31/Colossians 3:1f/2 Thessalonians 1). Over and over again, the NT shows that the parousia of Christ would be the humiliation of the enemies of Christ and the vindication and glorification of the followers of Christ. This is Romans 8: "The suffering of this present time" would give way to "the manifestation of the sons of God." They would go from shame to glory!

Thus, to the first–century saints, both individually and corporately, the persecuted, the despised, the ostracized body of shame of which they were members, the destruction of their persecutors would be a glorious event to be sure!

The once humiliated Messiah who had "humbled himself, and became obedient to death, even the death of the Cross" (Philippians 2:5f) would come "in the glory of the Father" (Matthew 16:27). He would come in power and great glory (Matthew 24:30f). He would come in righteous judgment, turning the tables on the persecutors of his followers: "It is a righteous thing with God to repay with tribulation, those who are troubling you." This would be in the day in which he would come to be "glorified in his saints" and the life and the glory that was "hidden" would be revealed (Colossians 3:1–3)!

To those early Christians, oppressed, hated, ostracized and persecuted, the fall of Jerusalem—the destruction of the persecuting power— was an amazing vindication and glorification of the Lord they served, and modern Christians should view that event in the same way.

How Could Jesus Call the Message of the Impending Fall of Jerusalem, the Gospel (the "Good News!") of the Kingdom?

Point # 3

The Removal of the Old Covenant World Was The Full Bloom of the New Creation

How could Jesus describe the coming fall of Jerusalem as "this gospel of the kingdom"? That was going to be—and was—horrific! And yet, when one considers that event in light of the OT prophecies of the New Creation, it becomes increasingly evident why and how Jesus could describe the coming dissolution of the Temple and the City as "this gospel (good news) of the kingdom." For brevity, I will only consider one Old Covenant prophecy of the coming New Creation, Isaiah 65.

Thus says the Lord:

> As the new wine is found in the cluster, And one says, 'Do not destroy it, For a blessing is in it,' So will I do for My servants' sake, That I may not destroy them all. I will bring forth descendants from Jacob, And from Judah an heir of My mountains; My elect shall inherit it, And My servants shall dwell there. Sharon shall be a fold of flocks, And the Valley of Achor a place for herds to lie down, For My people who have sought Me. "But you are those who forsake the Lord, Who forget My holy mountain, Who prepare a table for Gad, And who furnish a drink offering for Meni. Therefore I will number you for the sword, And you shall all bow down to the slaughter; Because, when I called, you did not answer; When I spoke, you did not hear, But did evil before My eyes, And chose that in which I do not

20

delight." Therefore thus says the Lord God: "Behold, My servants shall eat, But you shall be hungry; Behold, My servants shall drink, But you shall be thirsty; Behold, My servants shall rejoice, But you shall be ashamed; Behold, My servants shall sing for joy of heart, But you shall cry for sorrow of heart, And wail for grief of spirit. You shall leave your name as a curse to My chosen; For the Lord God will slay you, And call His servants by another name; So that he who blesses himself in the earth Shall bless himself in the God of truth; And he who swears in the earth Shall swear by the God of truth; Because the former troubles are forgotten, And because they are hidden from My eyes. For behold, I create new heavens and a new earth; And the former shall not be remembered or come to mind. But be glad and rejoice forever in what I create; For behold, I create Jerusalem as a rejoicing, And her people a joy. I will rejoice in Jerusalem, And joy in My people; The voice of weeping shall no longer be heard in her, Nor the voice of crying."

There is little doubt that Isaiah 65 is a pivotally important prophecy for the NT writers. Paul cites it to justify his mission to the Gentiles as a result of the unbelief of the Jews (Romans 10:20–21). It likewise serves as one of the sources for the doctrine of the salvation of the remnant (65:8). Both Peter and John cite Isaiah 65 in their predictions of the New Heavens and Earth (2 Peter 3/Revelation 21).

But notice that in Isaiah 65, YHVH is emphatic that the marvelous New Creation would come at the time of the destruction of the Old Covenant World, when "the Lord God will slay you" (65:13). A quick anecdote.

Some years ago, on PalTalk, I was engaged in a discussion with a

21

Jewish rabbi. We were discussing Jesus as Messiah and the creation of the New Covenant people. I made a comment, without immediately documenting it, that even the Old Covenant foretold the end of Old Covenant Israel. The rabbi was immediately incensed and challenged that statement (rather acrimoniously, I might add). He demanded to know the ground for my comment. I read Isaiah 65:13: "The Lord God will slay you." He grew even more agitated and said, "to slay does not mean to kill or destroy!" When I challenged him to document that rather amazing claim with some proof, he disappeared from the discussion. The very fact that he would claim that to be slain does not mean to kill or destroy was more than sufficient proof to prove that he was beyond desperate.

So, in Isaiah 65, we find the following:

O The declaration of Israel's rebellion, and the consequent prophecy that the Lord would punish her, and call the Gentiles, a people that did not know Him, to Himself.

OThe promise of the salvation of a remnant.

O The promise of the Messianic Banquet, i.e. "My servants shall eat, my servants shall drink", etc.. This is a resurrection prophecy (cf. Isaiah 25:6–8)!

O The promise—threat—that He would ultimately destroy the Nation, "The Lord God shall slay you, and call His people by another name."

O The promise of the New Creation, the New Heavens and Earth, the New Jerusalem.

O The proclamation that when the New Creation arrived, the Old would "no longer be remembered."

22

A full discussion of this fantastic prophecy is beyond the scope of this book. However, what I want to show is that the destruction of Old Covenant Israel—which meant the destruction of the City—would be the foundation for the arrival of the New Creation. Just like the promise of the New Creation demanded the destruction of the Old (it shall not be remembered or come to mind), the New Jerusalem called for the destruction of the Old. So, when the Lord promised to create a New Jerusalem, this implied the destruction of the Old City, *and that is Matthew 24.*

There is an important point here. All three futurist views of eschatology posit the end of the age, with the attendant judgment, coming of the Lord, the resurrection *and the New Creation* at the end of the Christian age. Not one of them posits the destruction of the church at the so–called "end of time." Not one of them says that God will "slay" the church and create a new people with a new name at the end of the current Christian age!

Do you catch the incredible power of this?

Isaiah 65 is the key source of the NT predictions of the coming New Creation! 2 Peter 3 and Revelation draw directly from it. Well, if Isaiah 65 is the source and ground of the New Testament predictions of the coming New Creation, and if Isaiah 65 does not predict the coming destruction of the church as the people of God, with the attendant creation of a new people with a new name, then it is patently wrong to say that the New Creation anticipated by the New Testament writers was a prediction of the coming end of time foretold by Isaiah. In other words, if Isaiah did not predict the end of the Christian age, it is wrong to apply 2 Peter 3 and Revelation to some end of the Christian age since they were both looking for the fulfillment of Isaiah. And there is more.

If the eschatology that you proclaim does not teach that the New Creation comes at the time of the destruction of the Old World of

Israel ("the Lord God shall slay you") then you are teaching a different eschatology from that of Isaiah. If you reject the idea that the New Creation only comes at the time of the destruction of Old Covenant Israel, you are rejecting the words of Isaiah. Given the fact that the NT writers are emphatic that their eschatological hope was *nothing* but what was foretold by the OT prophets, (cf. Acts 3:23f) this means that unless you can produce some OT prophecy of the destruction of literal, material "heaven and earth" and the creation of another physical "heaven and earth"—all of which is different from Isaiah 65–66—then your eschatology is false.

Some commentators seek to avoid this conundrum by claiming that while Isaiah 65 was about AD 70, the first–century catastrophe was a type or shadow of the yet future end of the age. This was the view of Joel McDurmon in our 2012 formal public debate.[15] McDurmon wrote an article in preparation for that debate, and in that article, he made the following claim:

> While 2 Peter 3:13 is definitely related thematically to Isaiah 65, it is a mistake to think that there is an exclusive relationship between the Isaiah passage and any New Testament usage, as if Isaiah were giving a unique prophecy of a unique event in the future, and then Peter and John were announcing the fulfillment of that one predicted event on their horizon (or at any time in the future). It is not that Isaiah announced "X," and that Peter and John were saying "the time has come for X," after which time "X" is done and gone.[16]

---

[15] A book of that debate, as well as DVDs or Mp3s, are available from my websites, Amazon and Kindle.

McDurmon, who follows in the footsteps of other Postmillennial writers, was claiming that while 2 Peter and Revelation contain similar themes and is related to Isaiah, that in reality, 2 Peter 3 and Revelation are not predicting what Isaiah 65 predicted! Of course, that is a rejection of the words of Peter who said: "according to his promise, we look for a new heavens and a new earth" (2 Peter 3:13). Peter was in fact looking for what Isaiah predicted.

How does all of this relate to our question, How could Jesus call the coming destruction of Jerusalem the 'gospel (good news) of the kingdom'? The answer is quite simple, and yet, it is overlooked or ignored by the vast majority of commentators. That coming destruction was "good news" because the end of the Old World was to be the full arrival of the New World! (This totally falsifies the horrid "Israel Only" false doctrine!).

In Isaiah, the "death" of the Old Covenant people would give birth to the new people with the new name. Was that bad news? Well, from one perspective, of course it was, because the new people could not be created until the old people were slain! This is a bad news/good news scenario!

In Isaiah, the end of the Old Creation would give rise to the New in which LIFE and blessings would abound! This is—when properly considered—a stark contrast with the Old. Under the Old, sin and death reigned. But, in the New Creation, life is the key element! What wondrous news!

---

[16] You can read some of McDurmon's claims in regard to 2 Peter 3 here: https://americanvision.org/5523/the-promise-of-his-appearing-2-peter-3/.

In Isaiah, we are told that the Old Creation would no longer be "remembered." The word that is translated as "remembered" is *zakar*, and carries with it tremendous covenantal connotations. Jason Meyer calls attention to this: "'Remember' is a common term associated with covenants. It does not mean that God forgets and needs a reminder. The verb could be idiomatically rendered 'to act in order to fulfill the covenantal oath or obligations."[17] Meyer was not commenting on Isaiah, but, his observation is valid nonetheless. See my discussion of "remember" in my *Who Is This Babylon?* book. This is a very important issue.

What this means is that when the Lord said that the first "heaven and earth" (and by implication, the first Jerusalem) would no longer be *remembered*, He was saying that the first creation would lose its covenantal standing! It would no longer be "remembered" before the Lord in the same covenantal sense. This is just a way of saying that the Old Covenant Creation would pass away, to give way to the *New Covenant Creation!* It proves that the Old Creation was *a covenant creation.* And, the New Creation would be everlasting. It would never pass away (Isaiah 66/Matthew 24:35)!

It is indisputably true that Isaiah 65 predicted the New Creation. It posited that New World at the time of the passing of the Old Jerusalem. It shows that the Old Creation was a covenant creation. It is not focused on material, physical creation!

Given the fact that the NT writers draw directly from Isaiah 65 to speak of the events taking place in their lifetime, and events that they said were at hand and coming soon (Revelation 22:6f) one has the right to suggest that they were—as they say they were—anticipating the imminent fulfillment of Isaiah 65. And that means that they knew

---

[17] Jason Meyer, *The End of the Law*, NAC Studies in Bible and Theology, (Nashville, TN; B and H Academic, 2009), 245, n. 41.

that horrific days were ahead. But, they likewise knew that the "birth pangs" of Messiah would give way to the everlasting kingdom of Christ, the New Covenant World of Jesus, where life and righteousness are the order of the day. That was the best of "good news."

I suggest that what we have in Isaiah 65 and Matthew 24 are parallel passages. Jesus' prediction in Matthew 24 is drawing from the Old Testament predictions like Isaiah 65–66. (There are echoes of Isaiah in the Olivet Discourse to be sure). In the Tanakh, there is the repeated, emphatic narrative that the New Creation would come at the time of the termination of the Old Covenant World of Israel. Jesus was obviously knowledgeable of this.

While the prediction of the destruction of the Old Covenant people was a terrible reality, the brighter, ultimate truth is that the passing of the Old World would give full bloom to the New—just as Hebrews 8:6–13 suggests. And the New Covenant World was to be—and it is! —so far greater than the Old Creation that the passing of the Old could be described as "this gospel of the kingdom."

Be sure to get a copy of my book, *The Elements Shall Melt With Fervent Heat,* for a fuller discussion of the passing of Old Covenant Jerusalem and the Temple as the passing away of the Old Covenant "heaven and earth." That book is available from my websites, Amazon, Kindle and other retailers.

How Could Jesus Call the Message of the Impending Fall of Jerusalem, the Gospel (the "Good News!") of the Kingdom?

Point # 4

The Time of the Fall of Jerusalem Was The Time of the Regathering/Restoration of Israel (Mt. 24:31)

One thing that is undeniable from the Olivet Discourse and Jesus' prediction of the coming end of the age is that at that time, *the gathering of the elect* would take place (24:31):

"And He will send His angels with a great sound of a trumpet, and they will gather together His elect from the four winds, from one end of heaven to the other."

Here we have the coming of Christ as the Son of Man, sending out his angels at the sounding of the Great Trumpet, for the gathering of the saints.

Thus, in some way, in some manner, we must admit that Matthew 24 is about the in–gathering, the gathering of God's elect. Needless to say, the nature and identity of this gathering is hotly disputed, but, the fact that Jesus was speaking of the gathering is indisputable.

To note that the ingathering is an eschatological motif is to state the obvious. What is important to realize is that what Jesus was predicting was the climax of Israel's covenant history, the "restoration of Israel" that would lead to the salvation of the nations.

Throughout the Tanakh, the story of God's end–time gathering is a constant theme. It is the story of the "Second Exodus" of Isaiah 11. It is the gathering from the east and the west of the children of God scattered abroad (Isaiah 43:5). What is fascinating in this latter text is that Jesus "widens" the perspective from just Israel to the Gentiles.

Speaking to Israel about the faith of the Centurion, a pagan, Jesus promised that "many shall come from the east and the west and sit down with Abraham, Isaac, and Jacob in the kingdom" (Matthew 8:11–12). He was thus including those like the Centurion, who were not of Israel, in those to be gathered into the kingdom. This is confirmed by taking a look at some of the other OT prophecies of the end–time gathering.

For brevity, we will look at just one of many texts, Isaiah 56:1–12:

> Do not let the son of the foreigner Who has joined himself to the Lord Speak, saying, "The Lord has utterly separated me from His people"; Nor let the eunuch say, "Here I am, a dry tree." For thus says the Lord: "To the eunuchs who keep My Sabbaths, And choose what pleases Me, And hold fast My covenant, Even to them I will give in My house And within My walls a place and a name Better than that of sons and daughters; I will give them an everlasting name That shall not be cut off. Also the sons of the foreigner Who join themselves to the Lord, to serve Him, And to love the name of the Lord, to be His servants— Everyone who keeps from defiling the Sabbath, And holds fast My covenant—Even them I will bring to My holy mountain, And make them joyful in My house of prayer. Their burnt offerings and their sacrifices Will be accepted on My altar; For My house shall be called a house of prayer for all nations." The Lord God, who gathers the outcasts of Israel, says, "Yet I will gather to him Others besides those who are gathered to him."

The context is that the ten northern tribes had been scattered among—"swallowed up"—among the nations (Hosea 8:8). But, the Lord looked to the time when Israel would be "restored/regathered" (In the LXX

29

the word for *gather* is from *sunagogee*, v. 8, and Jesus used a compound cognate of this in Matthew 24:31, where he used *episunagogee*).

The word sunagogee and its cognates is an important eschatological word in the LXX. This is a very distinctive and powerful word. While the word can be used in a somewhat "mundane" sense of gathering of people (or even animals), it is also used in the LXX (The Greek translation of the Hebrew Old Testament) to speak of the eschatological gathering of Israel under Messiah in the kingdom. Or, the idea conveyed in *sunagogee* and cognates is expressed in terms such as the Lord's return to His people after His departure. Let me illustrate from Hosea 5:15; 6:1–3:

> I will return again to My place till they acknowledge their offense. Then they will seek My face; In their affliction they will earnestly seek Me. Come, and let us return to the Lord; for He has torn, but He will heal us; He has stricken, but He will bind us up. After two days He will revive us; on the third day He will raise us up, that we may live in His sight. Let us know, let us pursue the knowledge of the Lord. His going forth is established as the morning; He will come to us like the rain.

Take note of the following:

1. Due to Israel's sin, YHVH departed. Now, it is patently obvious that this was not a physical, bodily departure.

2. Israel said that she would return to the Lord. This is likewise not a physical return, (or rapture) but a covenantal return, a return to obedience of the Lord's word.

3. Israel expresses her faith that if she repents, "He will come to us."

30

This is the return of the Lord, but, once again, there is no visible, literal, bodily coming of the Lord.

In Hosea 2:15f, that return and restoration is posited under the imagery of the Lord gathering Israel to "the valley of Achor," making the New Covenant with her, and remarrying her (Hosea 2:18f).

So, the idea of the gathering and the idea of the return of the Lord are inter–connected with one another.

This departure, repentance and return/gathering motif is found throughout the Tanakh. Notice Malachi 3:7—"Return to Me, and I will return to you."

Ezekiel 37 also contains one of the key Messianic "gathering" promises. In the famous vision of the valley of dry bones, the Lord promised to restore "the whole house of Israel" (i.e. all twelve tribes) under the Messiah and the New Covenant.

Ezekiel 37:21

> Then say to them, "Thus says the Lord God: 'Surely I will take the children of Israel from among the nations, wherever they have gone, and will gather them from every side and bring them into their own land.'"

The word *sunagogee* and cognates is used many times in Ezekiel to speak of the Lord gathering the "Jews" into Jerusalem for judgment at the hands of Babylon (Ezekiel 22), the literal return/gathering from Babylonian captivity back to the land of Israel (chapter 11), and the ultimate eschatological gathering of the whole house of Israel to Messiah her king (36–37).

What is so significant about Ezekiel 37 and the promise of the gathering of Israel "into the land" is that at that time, the Lord would establish His tabernacle among them, and dwell with them (Ezekiel 37:26). And Paul, whose eschatological hope was nothing but the hope of Israel found in the OT prophets, *quotes directly from this very verse* to say that the church of the living God is that promised tabernacle (2 Corinthians 6:16): "You are the temple of God, as it is written...". This means, can only mean, one thing: Israel was being "regathered"!

Notice now Isaiah 27:9–13:

> Therefore by this the iniquity of Jacob will be covered; And this is all the fruit of taking away his sin: When he makes all the stones of the altar Like chalkstones that are beaten to dust, Yet the fortified city will be desolate, The habitation forsaken and left like a wilderness; There the calf will feed, and there it will lie down And consume its branches. When its boughs are withered, they will be broken off; The women come and set them on fire. For it is a people of no understanding; Therefore He who made them will not have mercy on them, And He who formed them will show them no favor. And it shall come to pass in that day That the Lord will thresh, From the channel of the River to the Brook of Egypt; And you will be gathered one by one, O you children of Israel. So it shall be in that day: The great trumpet will be blown; They will come, who are about to perish in the land of Assyria, And they who are outcasts in the land of Egypt, And shall worship the Lord in the holy mount at Jerusalem. (I will have more to say on Isaiah 27 and the resurrection later in this work).

There is so much here! But notice some bullet points:

Isaiah 27 is part of the "Little Apocalypse" (Isaiah 24–27) as the scholars call it. It is called this because it is so focused on the end–time salvation, resurrection, restoration, kingdom. And the NT writers cite, echo, allude to these chapters repeatedly in their predictions of the last days, the resurrection, the kingdom and the salvation of Israel—the regathering and restoration of Israel.

. - This is a prophecy of the salvation of Israel, "Therefore by this the iniquity of Jacob will be covered." It is important to realize that Paul cites these very verses in Romans 11:25–27 in his prediction of the then future to him salvation of Israel at the coming of the Lord. See my in–depth discussion of this connection in my *Elijah Has Come: A Solution to Romans 11:25–27.*

. - The Lord says that Israel's salvation would come *through judgment*—"When he makes all the stones of the altar Like chalkstones that are beaten to dust, Yet the fortified city will be desolate, The habitation forsaken and left like a wilderness."

. - The people whom the Lord had created would no longer find mercy (v. 11): "For it is a people of no understanding; Therefore He who made them will not have mercy on them, And He who formed them will show them no favor." This is a direct echo of Deuteronomy 32:28 which is a prediction of Israel's last days! Thus, Isaiah is speaking of Israel's ultimate fate, her last days judgment and salvation.

. - And notice now that it would be "at that time" or "in that day" which is the day of the judgment of Jerusalem and the Temple,

> And it shall come to pass in that day That the Lord will thresh, From the channel of the River to the Brook of Egypt; And you will be gathered one by one, O you children of Israel. So it shall be in that day: The great trumpet will be blown; They will come, who are about to perish in the land of Assyria,

And they who are outcasts in the land of Egypt, And shall worship the Lord in the holy mount at Jerusalem. (v. 12–13).

Do you catch that? At the time of the Lord's coming in judgment of Jerusalem and the Temple, the time of Israel's salvation, the "great trumpet" would sound for the gathering of the people!

It should be noted that the rabbis and the scholars are agreed that Isaiah 27:12–13 was a prediction of the end–time ingathering—the resurrection.

Mitch and Zhava Glaser say, "The holy one, Blessed be He, will sound the shofar at the time of the ingathering of the exiles of Israel to their place (Isaiah 27:13)"[18]

Greg Beale, commenting on 1 Corinthians 15:52 and the sounding of the trumpet at the time of the resurrection says that 1 Corinthians 15 is an echo of Isaiah 27:13.[19] The implications of this are staggering!

John Nolland, also says that Matthew 24:31 is drawing on Zechariah 9:14 and Isaiah 27:13.[20]

---

[18] Mitch and Zhava Glaser, *The Fall Feasts of Israel*, Chicago; Moody Press, 1987), 22, 23—citing Eliyahu Zuta 2).

[19] Gregory Beale, *Commentary on the New Testament Use of the OT*, (Grand Rapids; Baker Academic, Apollos, 2007), 747.

[20] John Nolland, *New International Greek Text Commentary, Matthew*, (Grand Rapids; Eerdmans, Paternoster, 2005), 985.

Donald Hagner says,

> The reference to the blowing of the Great Trumpet in connection with the gathering of the righteous is found in Isaiah 27:13 (in the NT reference to the eschatological trumpet occurs in conjunction with the descent from heaven in 1 Thessalonians 4:16; there, as in 1 Corinthians 15:52 the trumpet is associated with the resurrection of the dead, which Matthew makes no mention of here.[21]

Hagner exhibits a common, but troubling hermeneutic here. He implies that since Jesus (Matthew) in Matthew 24:31 does not explicitly mention the resurrection, that this means that the resurrection is not in view. This is specious and far removed from the ancient Hebraic mind–set. The idea that because specific words, terms or phrases are not used in a given text means that a doctrine is not present is just bad hermeneutic! The ancient Hebrews and rabbis simply did not think like that! See my series of articles addressing this hermeneutic, which was employed by Joel McDurmon in our formal public debate in 2012. That series of articles is on my websites.

Now, if it is true that Matthew 24:31 is drawing on the prophecy of Isaiah 27—and there can be little doubt of this—the implications are staggering!

That connection is established by a brief comparison of the two prophecies:

Isaiah 27 is actually a prediction of the coming of the Lord to avenge the blood of the martyrs. See Isaiah 26:19–21. Needless to say,

---

[21] Donald Hagner, *Word Biblical Commentary, Matthew 14-28, Vol. 33b*, (Dallas; Word Publishers, 1995), 714.

the context of Matthew 24 is Jesus' prediction of the avenging of all the blood of all the righteous, all the way back to creation—in the judgment of Jerusalem.

Isaiah 27 is thus a prediction of the judgment of Jerusalem and the Temple, just like Matthew 23–24 was a prediction of the judgment of Jerusalem and the Temple.

Isaiah 27 predicted the sounding of the Trumpet for the gathering (*sunago*) and Jesus predicted the gathering of the elect (*episunagogee*) at the sounding of the Great Trumpet.

Isaiah 27 is actually a prediction of the resurrection since the reference is to "those who are perishing" those in "captivity" and thus, they were considered "dead." Thus, Matthew 24:31 was a prophecy of the resurrection! Jesus was unequivocal in positing the fulfillment of these things for his generation (24:34). That means that Matthew 24:31 was a prediction of the resurrection that would occur in Jesus' generation!

All of this means that, as we have suggested, the impending judgment on Jerusalem and the Temple was both a good news/bad news scenario. The bad news was that the Old Covenant world had to be destroyed, just as Isaiah 27 foretold when it spoke of the destruction of the "fortified city" and the destruction of the altar of the Temple. And yet, in the midst of that catastrophe was the promise of the removal of Israel's sin, her "regathering" to the Lord, i.e. the restoration of the fellowship that had been lost through her rebellion and sin.

This is the very situation Jesus described in Matthew 24. He foretold the coming Abomination of Desolation, with the resultant Great Tribulation, followed by his coming on the clouds of heaven in power and great glory, *at the sounding of the Great Trumpet to restore and regather the saints*! The Olivet Discourse is Isaiah 27 restated and interpreted by the Lord himself.

Jesus' application of Isaiah 27 (and Paul's application of Ezekiel 37) demands a rejection of the literalistic hermeneutic of the Dispensational world—and a surprising number of former preterists! The fact that Jesus posited the fulfillment of Isaiah 27 for his generation demands a rejection of that sort of literalism. Jesus was not saying that (just like Ezekiel 37 was not saying) that there was to be a literal physical restoration of Israel to the physical land. That is patently not what those prophecies—as interpreted by the NT writers—foretold. Israel, alienated from God just like Adam had been, would be restored to God through Messiah Jesus and the New Covenant, bringing that Old Covenant world to its end. I will develop this further just below as I examine Isaiah 52, a marvelous prophecy of the end–time "gathering" of Israel under Messiah in the New Creation.

Don't forget that later in this work, I will show that the time of the fall of Jerusalem was to be the time of the *resurrection*. That is one of the major reasons why Jesus could call that impending judgment the "gospel of the kingdom." There is no better news than resurrection life!

A Closer Look At the Gathering

As just seen, the distinctive words (*episunago*/*episunagogee*) that are used in Matthew 24 (and in the OT) to speak of the gathering at the Lord's coming are used in the Tanakh to speak of the eschatological gathering to the Lord at his coming and in the kingdom. I want now to look a bit closer at the concept of the gathering in the OT.

While this study alone could be quite lengthy, I want now to explore another great OT prophecy of the end–times gathering. That text is Isaiah 52:1–12:

Awake, awake! Put on your strength, O Zion; Put on your beautiful garments, O Jerusalem, the holy city! For the uncircumcised and the unclean Shall no longer come to you. Shake yourself from the dust, arise; Sit down, O Jerusalem! Loose yourself from the bonds of your neck, O captive daughter of Zion! For thus says the Lord: "You have sold yourselves for nothing, And you shall be redeemed without money." For thus says the Lord God: "My people went down at first Into Egypt to dwell there; Then the Assyrian oppressed them without cause. Now therefore, what have I here," says the Lord, "That My people are taken away for nothing? Those who rule over them Make them wail," says the Lord, "And My name is blasphemed continually every day. Therefore My people shall know My name; Therefore they shall know in that day That I am He who speaks: 'Behold, it is I.'" How beautiful upon the mountains Are the feet of him who brings good news, Who proclaims peace, Who brings glad tidings of good things, Who proclaims salvation, Who says to Zion, "Your God reigns!" Your watchmen shall lift up their voices, With their voices they shall sing together; For they shall see eye to eye When the Lord brings back Zion. Break forth into joy, sing together, You waste places of Jerusalem! For the Lord has comforted His people, He has redeemed Jerusalem. The Lord has made bare His holy arm In the eyes of all the nations; And all the ends of the earth shall see The salvation of our God. Depart! Depart! Go out from there, Touch no unclean thing; Go out from the midst of her, Be clean, You who bear the vessels of the Lord. For you shall not go out with haste, Nor go by flight; For the Lord will go before you, And the God of Israel will be your rear guard.

We need to point out that in verse 12, the literal rendering in the LXX is that "the God of Israel will *gather* you." The word *episunagogee* is used there. (I am not sure why *episunagogee* is not translated in many translations, unless they are following the Masoretic text, which is possible).

Now, don't forget that this is the word, *episunagogee,* used by Jesus—the Messiah—in Matthew 23:37 and Matthew 24:31—with a cognate used in 25:31f. Jesus was not using this word lightly or in isolation from the eschatological expectations and hopes of his audience. They well knew that the OT prophets had spoken of the coming last days gathering, at the coming of the Lord, the judgment and the resurrection—in the eternal kingdom. It is a strange and specious hermeneutic to suggest or believe that Jesus was contemplating a literal, physical, end of time gathering when the OT prophetic source of the "gathering" hope had nothing to do with such an event.[22]

Notice some of the elements of this wonderful text of Isaiah 52:

1. Verse 1 is an implicit prophecy of the resurrection. Israel is called upon to rise from the dust. This imagery—and it is imagery—of

---

[22] It is more than apparent also that Jesus was not speaking of a literal rapture of the saints off of the earth, as posited by Ed Stevens of the International Preterist Association. Stevens and I engaged in a formal written debate on the issue of whether there was a literal gathering/rapture in AD 70—with Stevens affirming that there was. Through three affirmations, I took note of the covenantal nature of Jesus' discussion of the gathering and how a literal rapture was never in view. Stevens refused to address the arguments claiming they were "irrelevant." This is amazing since our propositions were about whether there was a literal rapture. I repeatedly asked him how my arguments on the rapture could be irrelevant, since our debate was on the rapture. At the time of this writing he has refused to offer any answer at all.

coming out of the dust is a well known Hebraic metaphoric and apocalyptic resurrection motif. It does not refer to a literal rising out of the literal dust, but rather out of a condition of humiliation, defeat, dishonor. See our previous discussion of the shame–v–honor motif in the Scriptures.

2. The text is also a prophecy of the "remarriage" of Israel. Isaiah was a contemporary of Hosea. The putting on of her "beautiful garments" is a reference to the Wedding Garments. In both Isaiah (51–54) and Hosea, the Lord affirmed His past marriage to Israel, but that due to their spiritual adultery, He had divorced her (Hosea 2:1–2). Yet, He promised that in the last days, under "David" their king (Hosea 3), He would remarry them, making a New Covenant with them (Hosea 2:18–23).

3. It is likewise a prophecy of the New Jerusalem, the redeemed Zion. The promise is that when the redemption takes place, the uncircumcised and the unclean would not enter. (This makes one wonder if this passage served as part of the justification of the Judaizers, who accepted Christ as the promised Messiah, but, insisted that in order to be "in him" one had to be circumcised! I suggest reading Colossians 2:11–13 in light of this prophecy and in the light of the controversy over circumcision). This vision of the New Zion is nothing less than a vision of the New Jerusalem of Revelation 21:1f.

4. Verse 7 helps us identify, with certainty, the time of the fulfillment of this prophecy: "How beautiful upon the mountains Are the feet of him who brings good news, Who proclaims peace, Who brings glad tidings of good things, Who proclaims salvation, Who says to Zion, 'Your God reigns!'" This is a *crux interpretum* since Paul in Romans 10:14f cites this passage verbatim to speak of the first century proclamation of the Gospel! Paul applied Isaiah 52 to the then on–going proclamation of the Gospel! This virtually demands, therefore, that we see the promise of the resurrection, the Re–Marriage, the Redemption of Zion—the Gathering—as to be

40

fulfilled in the first century. It is entirely inappropriate to deny Paul's application.

5. Notice that Isaiah was proclaiming the coming of the Kingdom at this time of redemption. The message was to be proclaimed was "Your God reigns!" This means that the "Gospel of the Kingdom" was the message of Israel's salvation—which, as we have seen, would result in salvation flowing to the nations.

6. The prophecy likewise provides the source for what Jesus said would be done in his generation. He said that the "Gospel of the Kingdom" would be preached into all the world for a witness to the nations (Matthew 24:14). Likewise, Isaiah said that the message of salvation and the reigning of the Lord ("Your God reigns!"—the Kingdom) would be proclaimed into all the world: "The Lord has made bare His holy arm In the eyes of all the nations; and all the ends of the earth shall see the salvation of our God." (Isaiah 52:10) This is nothing but the promise that the Gospel of the Kingdom would be preached into all the world.

Paul is emphatic in his epistles, written in the late AD 50s and AD 60s, that Jesus' words—and thus, the prophecy of Isaiah—had been—was being—fulfilled. Even in Romans 10, after citing Isaiah 52, he says that the Gospel had been proclaimed into the whole world. In Titus 2:12f, in Colossians 1, etc., Paul undeniably affirmed the fulfillment of the World Mission. See my book, *Into All the World, Then Comes the End*, for a full discussion of Jesus' promise in Matthew 24:14. There can literally be no doubt that the World Mission was fulfilled in the first century.

7. Verse 11 also gives confirmation that the prophecy was being fulfilled in the first century. The redeemed of the Lord (which would be the righteous remnant) are called upon to be holy: "Depart! Depart! Go out from there, Touch no unclean thing; Go out from the midst of her, Be clean!" Just as Paul cited Isaiah 52 as the ground of his Gentile Mission and the preaching of the Gospel to Israel of his day, in 2

Corinthians 6:16f, as he wrote to the church at Corinth, he cites this verse verbatim to remind them that they were the promised Messianic Temple, and that as a result of this, they were to be holy! We, therefore, have the Apostle citing Isaiah 52 verbatim to speak of what was happening in his day, his time, his ministry. And that can only mean that the time of redemption, the time of salvation, the time of the kingdom had arrived.

8. As noted above, in verse 12, we find the great prophecy of the gathering. Instead of the text saying that the Lord would be their rearguard, in the LXX, it is, "the Lord your God will gather (*episunagogee*) you."

Several things are apparent from the above, and make no mistake, we could have expanded the points to be discussed. Isaiah 52 is a marvelous prophecy! But, based on what we have seen, we can draw some conclusions.

A. Since the NT writers apply Isaiah 52 to their day, their times, as being fulfilled, then it is incumbent that we honor and accept their declarations.

B. That means that the salvation of Israel, including the resurrection, Israel's restoration, was to be fulfilled in the first century.

C. It means that the establishment of the kingdom was in the first century. Isaiah 52 is a devastating refutation and falsification of Dispensationalism! When Paul applied Isaiah 52 to his day and his ministry, saying it was being fulfilled, we must remember that the message that Paul was proclaiming, i.e. Isaiah 52—was "Our God reigns!"

D. Since Isaiah 52 was being fulfilled in the first century, this means, unequivocally, that the Gathering of Israel was underway! God said that in the day of redemption of Zion, the time of her resurrection, the time of her remarriage, was to be the time when He would gather her.

Remember that one of Jesus' favorite themes and topics was the marriage (remarriage) of Israel (Matthew 22/Luke 14) as well as the resurrection. In addition, Jesus declared that it was his desire to gather Israel (*episunagogee*) but, she refused (Matthew 23:37). Even though she—as the nation—refused to be gathered, he nonetheless said that the Gospel of the Kingdom would be preached into all the world, then, he would come on the clouds of heaven and "gather together" (*episunagogee*) the elect. He would "gather" the redeemed, his New Covenant bride, into his New Synagogue, his New Covenant gathering.

Is it not more than evident that Jesus never offered to gather Israel into one geographical location? While Dispensationalism says that 1948 was the beginning of the end–time gathering of Israel, with the restoration of Israel, this completely flies in the face of what Jesus said he wanted and tried to do in the first century. He wanted to gather (*episunagogee*) Israel.

Side Bar: It is important to see that Israel's sin prevented that "gathering" by and to Jesus. Yet, we are told that in spite of the fact that the vast majority of "Israel" that was restored in 1948 were "atheists, agnostics and unbelievers" that God did gather them!

The reality is that Jesus never, ever tried to gather his followers into one geographical location. But, he did try to gather people into a covenant relationship, fellowship, with him—"Come unto me all you that labor and are heavy laden, and I will give you rest" (Matthew 11:28f).

With these things in mind, it is easy to see how and why Jesus could call the message of the impending fall of Jerusalem—at the time of the gathering—as "the Gospel of the kingdom"? As we have noted, the message was indeed horrific on one hand, but, on the other hand, out of that catastrophic end would come the glorious, redeemed Zion, the New Jerusalem!

There is much, much more that could be said about this Isaiah 52, and about the "gathering"—which was the harvest and resurrection—but this is sufficient, I hope, to whet your appetite. When we reflect on Jesus' words in Matthew 24:14 in the light of the OT prophecies of the coming "gathering" (utilizing the distinctive Greek words of *sunagogee/episunagogee*), it should settle the issue of the time of the resurrection, the time of the coming of the Lord for salvation, the time of the kingdom. These things were to happen in the first century, with the passing of the Old Covenant world, epitomized by the Temple. To deny that the end of the Old Covenant age was to be considered as "the Gospel of the kingdom" is to deny the prophetic word.

How Could Jesus Call the Message of the Impending Fall of Jerusalem, the Gospel (the "Good News!") of the Kingdom?

Point # 5

It Was The Fulfillment of Key
Old Testament Eschatological Prophecies

As we just saw, no matter what else we might think of the Olivet Discourse, one thing is certain. Jesus linked the eschatological gathering (the good news of the kingdom) to that catastrophic end. He said that at his coming in that event, he would send out his angels and they would gather together the elect, from the four winds of the earth. This "gathering" (from *episunagogee*) was foretold by the OT prophets. It was the restoration of Israel, dead in sin, alienated from God due to her violation of the covenant.

Having examined Isaiah 52 as one of the key prophecies of the end–time gathering I want now to take a look at another important prophecy of the end–times gathering—Psalms 102:14–28:

> For Your servants take pleasure in her stones, And show favor to her dust. So the nations shall fear the name of the Lord, And all the kings of the earth Your glory. For the Lord shall build up Zion; He shall appear in His glory. He shall regard the prayer of the destitute, And shall not despise their prayer. This will be written for the generation to come, That a people yet to be created may praise the Lord. For He looked down from the height of His sanctuary; From heaven the Lord viewed the earth, To hear the groaning of the prisoner, To release those appointed to death, To declare the name of the Lord in Zion, And His praise in Jerusalem, When the peoples are gathered together, And the kingdoms, to serve the Lord. He weakened

my strength in the way; He shortened my days. I said, "O my God, Do not take me away in the midst of my days; Your years are throughout all generations. Of old You laid the foundation of the earth, And the heavens are the work of Your hands. They will perish, but You will endure; Yes, they will all grow old like a garment; Like a cloak You will change them, And they will be changed. But You are the same, And Your years will have no end. The children of Your servants will continue, And their descendants will be established before You."

✱ The Psalmist said that all the kings of the earth would glory at the work of the Lord, and that He would "appear in His glory."

✱ This prophecy is cited by Hebrews 1 to speak of the passing away of the Old Covenant "heavens and earth" versus the abiding, eternal nature of the New Covenant—and the age to come (2:5)—of Christ. It is clearly Messianic in nature, so let's take a look.

✱ There was to be, at the passing of the Old Creation, the creation of a New People: "a people yet to be created may praise the Lord." This is a massive problem for those who say that Psalms is talking about a so–called end of time, end of the Christian age event. Do those same people believe that the current people of God will be destroyed, for the Lord to create a New People? No, they do not. Thus, an appeal to Psalms 102 to prove a yet future end of time is not supported by this text.

✱ Notice that at the time of the creation of the new people, it would be a time of grace, mercy, and freedom: "From heaven the Lord viewed the earth, to hear the groaning of the prisoner, to release those appointed to death, to declare the name of the Lord in Zion, and His praise in Jerusalem." Needless to say, we have here a direct parallel with Isaiah 61:1–3:

46

The Spirit of the Lord God is upon Me, because the Lord has anointed Me to preach good tidings to the poor; He has sent Me to heal the brokenhearted, to proclaim liberty to the captives, and the opening of the prison to those who are bound; to proclaim the acceptable year of the Lord, and the day of vengeance of our God; to comfort all who mourn, to console those who mourn in Zion, to give them beauty for ashes, the oil of joy for mourning, the garment of praise for the spirit of heaviness; that they may be called trees of righteousness, the planting of the Lord, that He may be glorified.

Of course, the observant reader will recall immediately that in Luke 4, Jesus emphatically declared that the time for the fulfillment of Isaiah 61 had arrived. Thus, unless Psalms 102 and Isaiah 61 speak of two different times of salvation for Israel and the nations, then we have proof that both Psalms 102 and Isaiah 61 were to be fulfilled in the first century. And that brings us to the promise of the gathering.

In verse 22 the Lord spoke of that event: "When the peoples are gathered together, And the kingdoms, to serve the Lord."

The Psalmist used the word *episunagogee (in the LXX)* to speak of that eschatological gathering. It is important of course to pay particular note that it would not be just Israel that would be "gathered" but, the nations as well. This reminds us of Isaiah 56 where the Lord foretold that in the last days He would not only gather (*sunagogee*) Israel, but, he would gather nations "besides" Israel. Israel alone was never intended to be the exclusive focus of God's scheme of redemption. It was always God's plan to use Israel to bring salvation to the nations (Isaiah 49:6).

So, at the coming of the Lord in his glory, to redeem "Zion" and bring deliverance and freedom to the poor, the outcast and the prisoner, the

Lord would "gather together" (*episunagogee*) the outcasts of Israel as well as the nations.

This end–time gathering was the hope of Israel. It was nothing less than *the resurrection*, since the regathering of Israel from her sin— bondage—her alienation from God (cf. Ezekiel 37) was always considered to be "resurrection from the dead." To say that this was the promise of "good news" is a huge understatement. As N. T. Wright has cogently noted, what would happen to Israel would happen to the nations. The nations were dependent on what God would do for Israel:

> The fate of the nations was inexorably and irreversibly bound up with that of Israel...This point is of the utmost importance for the understanding of first–century Judaism and of emerging Christianity. What happens to the Gentiles is conditional upon, and conditioned by, what happens to Israel...The call of Israel has as its fundamental objective the rescue and restoration of the entire creation. Not to see this connection is to fail to understand the meaning of Israel's fundamental doctrines of monotheism and election. (Wright, 1996), 308).

In similar fashion, he wrote:

> "In many strands of Jewish expectation, demonstrably current in the first century, the fate of the Gentiles would hinge on the fate of Israel. What YHWH intended to do for the Gentiles, he would do in some sense or other through Israel."[23]

---

[23] N. T. Wright, *The New Testament and the People of God*, (Minneapolis; Fortress, 1992), 268.

So, what we find in Psalms 102 is a fantastic prophecy of the "restoration of Israel" the redemption of Zion, at the coming of the Lord in glory to gather the nations—this is the promise of the everlasting kingdom.

Of course, it takes but a moment of reflection to recall that Jesus foretold his coming in glory and salvation:

> For the Son of Man will come in the glory of His Father with His angels, and then He will reward each according to his works. Assuredly, I say to you, there are some standing here who shall not taste death till they see the Son of Man coming in His kingdom. (Matthew 16:27–28)

> Then the sign of the Son of Man will appear in heaven, and then all the tribes of the earth will mourn, and they will see the Son of Man coming on the clouds of heaven with power and great glory. 31 And He will send His angels with a great sound of a trumpet, and they will gather together (*episunagogee*) His elect from the four winds, from one end of heaven to the other (Matthew 24:30–31).

We have here many of the constituent elements of Psalms 102, just as we do in another passage in Matthew.

> When the Son of Man comes in His glory, and all the holy angels with Him, then He will sit on the throne of His glory. All the nations will be gathered (συναχθήσονται /*sunexthesetai*, a future indicative passive of *sunagogee*) before Him, and He will separate them one from another, as a shepherd divides his sheep from the goats. And He will set the sheep on His right hand, but the goats on the left. (Matthew 25:31–33).

49

So, just as in Psalms 102 (and the other two texts just cited) we have the coming of the Lord in glory, for the time of salvation and the kingdom, when the nations would be gathered.

Several things are certain from these passages and from the comments made earlier.

1. Jesus posited the fulfillment of these prophecies for the first century.

2. The gathering in view is not a physical gathering of all the nations into one geographical location as the graphic sermonizing lessons have portrayed this gathering. The gathering is *the bringing back into fellowship* the people that had been alienated/separated from God due to sin. It is the time of the creation of a New People, in a New Creation, where grace, mercy, salvation are the blessings of the kingdom rule of Messiah.

To suggest that Jesus did not have these eschatological "gathering" texts in mind is, I believe, to turn Matthew 24:30–31 on its head and to rob them of the soteriological glory that these verses deserve. When Jesus foretold the passing of the Old People, that was, to be sure, bad news. But, his reference to the end–time gathering meant that the promised salvation of the remnant in the kingdom of Messiah, and the extension of salvation to all the nations was to happen in that generation. This truly was "the good news of the kingdom" and that "good news" extends to us today, since we can participate in the salvation that came into full bloom at the passing of that Old Covenant world and covenant of sin and death.

How Could Jesus Call the Message of the Impending Fall of Jerusalem, the Gospel (the "Good News!") of the Kingdom?

Point # 6

The Fall of Jerusalem Was the Time of the Fulfillment of All Things
Answering Some Objections

How could the fall of Jerusalem be called the "gospel of the Kingdom?" I want to look at the idea that the end of the Old Covenant age, the fall of Jerusalem, was to be the time of the fulfillment of all eschatological prophecies. Needless to say this is a hotly contested claim, but, I am convinced that it is absolutely true. Notice the words of Jesus in Luke 21:22 as he described that coming catastrophe:

"These be the days of vengeance in which all things that are written must be fulfilled."

Now, on a surface reading of this passage it certainly appears that Jesus was saying that the events leading up to and consummating in the fall of Jerusalem would be the time of the final fulfillment of all eschatological prophecies. But, of course, this view is denied by all futurist views. There are about three or four "explanations" for Jesus' words that are offered to counter the idea that the fall of Jerusalem was the time when all prophecy would stand fulfilled.

Before examining those objections let me address a claim being made by former preterists, such as Sam Frost. In a recent FaceBook exchange, Frost claimed that preterists believe that all prophecy was fulfilled in AD 70. Sounds like what I am affirming, right? But, it is not even close to what I am and other preterists teach. What Frost is claiming is that preterists must believe, for instance, that the Virgin Birth was fulfilled at that time! In other words, Frost was claiming that preterists do not believe that *any* prophecy was fulfilled until AD 70. This claim is beyond ludicrous and ridiculous. It is patently false and Frost knows full well that his accusation is false. When I called him out on his false claim, he did not respond with a single keystroke.

Let me examine now the objections that are normally lodged against the claim that in the events leading up to and consummating in the destruction of Jerusalem, the process of fulfillment that had begun with John the Baptizer ("The law and the prophets were until John. Since then, the kingdom of God is proclaimed and all men press into it"—Luke 16:16) would be finalized. In those climactic events, the process of fulfillment would be completed and there would be no more eschatological prophecies to be fulfilled.

Naturally, as noted, objection is raised to this claim. I have encountered basically four major objections to the claim that all prophecy was fulfilled in the destruction of Jerusalem. I will briefly examine each of those objections.

Objection #1—All Does Not Mean Comprehensively "All"—Only the prophecies of the fall of Jerusalem were fulfilled.

First of all, (pun intended), it is to be admitted that the word "all" can be, and often is, qualified and limited. Context is king, and it is often the case where "all" refers to all of the things that refer to the subject at hand and not comprehensively "all." Undoubtedly, some will jump on this and say, "Preston has surrendered his argument, because he agrees that 'all' can be qualified/limited." It is more than obvious that in Luke 21, the discussion is about the fall of Jerusalem. That means that, "all things written" refers only to all of the prophecies concerning the fall of Jerusalem would be fulfilled at that time.

My response has been and is, "I agree that the context of Luke 21 is the judgment of Jerusalem! But, that means that the resurrection, the coming of the Lord and the judgment and kingdom has been fulfilled, because prophetically *all of those things* are inextricably linked with the fall of Jerusalem!" For brevity, I will give only a partial list of some of the texts that make this connection. In this brief list one should be able to see how the declaration of the coming destruction of Jerusalem in Jesus' generation could be called "this gospel of the kingdom."

A. Isaiah 25:1–9:

> O Lord, You are my God. I will exalt You, I will praise Your name, For You have done wonderful things; Your counsels of old are faithfulness and truth. For You have made a city a ruin, A fortified city a ruin, A palace of foreigners to be a city no more; It will never be rebuilt. Therefore the strong people will glorify You; The city of the terrible nations will fear You. For You have been a strength to the poor, A strength to the needy in his distress, A refuge from the storm, A shade from the heat; For the blast of the terrible ones is as a storm against the wall. You will reduce the noise of aliens, As heat in a dry place; As heat in the shadow of a cloud, The song of the terrible ones will be diminished. And in this mountain The Lord of hosts will make for all people A feast of choice pieces, A feast of wines on the lees, Of fat things full of marrow, Of well–refined wines on the lees. And He will destroy on this mountain The surface of the covering cast over all people, And the veil that is spread over all nations. He will swallow up death forever, And the Lord God will wipe away tears from all faces; The rebuke of His people He will take away from all the earth; For the Lord has spoken. And it will be said in that day: "Behold, this is our God; We have waited for Him, and He will save us. This is the

Lord; We have waited for Him; We will be glad and rejoice in His salvation."

I will only notice a few quick bullet points:

V—The time in view is the time of the resurrection (v. 8). This is surely the best of news!

V—"In that day" (v. 6), the Lord would create the Messianic Banquet on Mt. Zion. What wonderful news!

V—"In that Day" salvation would come—v. 9!

V—"In that Day," the fortified city and the temple would be totally destroyed (v. 1–3). This is the "bad news" the horrific news. On the one hand, Jerusalem and the temple, the center of Israel's world, would be destroyed. But, at that time, joy, gladness, salvation, and resurrection would be fulfilled!

B. Isaiah 26:16–19—

> Lord, in trouble they have visited You, They poured out a prayer when Your chastening was upon them. As a woman with child Is in pain and cries out in her pangs, When she draws near the time of her delivery, So have we been in Your sight, O Lord. We have been with child, we have been in pain; We have, as it were, brought forth wind; We have not accomplished any deliverance in the earth, Nor have the inhabitants of the world fallen. Your dead shall live; Together with my dead body they shall arise. Awake and sing, you who dwell in dust; For your dew is like the dew of herbs, And the earth shall cast out the dead.. For behold, the Lord comes out of His place To punish the inhabitants of the earth for their iniquity; The

earth will also disclose her blood, And will no more
cover her slain.

V—The passage speaks of the chastening of Israel, her "labor pains"
to bring forth salvation, all to no avail. Those labor pangs of Messiah,
as the scholars and the rabbis called them, are bound up with Israel's
last days (cf. Jeremiah 30:5f), and Jesus spoke of the labor pangs that
would take place in the first century prior to his coming in the fall of
Jerusalem (Matthew 24:8).

V—There is the prediction of resurrection (v. 19)—and as seen in
chapter 25, that is the time of salvation. It should be noted that in the
context of Isaiah 25–26 the "death" that is in view is the death of
nations. Israel saw herself as "in the dust" because of her exile and
punishment. She says that "other gods have ruled over us" but, speaks
confidently of the fact that "they are dead and shall never rise." (v.
13f). But, she also speaks confidently of how she will rise from the
dust; "Awake and sing, you who dwell in dust; For your dew is like
the dew of herbs, And the earth shall cast out the dead." The issue is
not human corpses in the dust, but rather the national "death" of exile
because of sin. See Ezekiel 37 as a parallel.

V—This time of deliverance would be at the coming of the Lord,
when the martyrs would be vindicated (v. 21). Jesus leaves no doubt
as to when all the blood, of all the martyrs would be vindicated. At his
coming in judgment against Jerusalem in his generation (Matthew
23:29f/24:29–31).

So, in Isaiah 26—and we have kept our comments on this chapter to
a bare minimum—we have the promise of the resurrection, the
promise of Israel's tribulation at the time of the coming of the Lord
to vindicate the martyrs, which Jesus posited for the time of the
destruction of Jerusalem.

C. Isaiah 27:9–13—

Therefore by this the iniquity of Jacob will be covered; And this is all the fruit of taking away his sin: When he makes all the stones of the altar Like chalkstones that are beaten to dust, Wooden images and incense altars shall not stand. Yet the fortified city will be desolate, The habitation forsaken and left like a wilderness; There the calf will feed, and there it will lie down And consume its branches. When its boughs are withered, they will be broken off; The women come and set them on fire. For it is a people of no understanding; Therefore He who made them will not have mercy on them, And He who formed them will show them no favor. And it shall come to pass in that day That the Lord will thresh, From the channel of the River to the Brook of Egypt; And you will be gathered one by one, O you children of Israel. So it shall be in that day: The great trumpet will be blown; They will come, who are about to perish in the land of Assyria, And they who are outcasts in the land of Egypt, And shall worship the Lord in the holy mount at Jerusalem.

V—I should note that in Isaiah 27:1–2, we are told that "in that day" which is the day of the Lord of chapter 26, the time of the resurrection and the coming of the Lord to vindicate the martyrs, that would be the time when the Lord would destroy "Leviathan" i.e. the Devil. This is, once again, the time of salvation (27:2f) when "the vineyard of the Lord" would be redeemed. The vineyard of the Lord was Israel (Isaiah 5).

V—Pay particular attention to verse 9—"By this the iniquity of Jacob will be covered; And this is all the fruit of taking away his sin: When he makes all the stones of the altar Like chalkstones that are beaten to dust." Here we have an emphatic declaration that Israel's sin would be taken away at the time of the destruction of the temple and the altar.

V—We are told that the reason for this coming judgment was: "For it is a people of no understanding; Therefore He who made them will not have mercy on them, And He who formed them will show them no favor." This passage is a direct echo of Deuteronomy 32:28. That chapter, Deuteronomy 32, is about Israel's last days (32:19f/29f). And the NT writers are very clear that they were living in the days foretold by Moses.

So, Isaiah 27 would be the fulfillment of Deuteronomy 32. Deuteronomy 32 is about Israel's last days. The NT writers apply Deuteronomy 32 to their day, to their generation. Therefore, the prophecy of Isaiah 27—the time of Israel's salvation, the time of the resurrection—was to be in the first century.

V—Notice now, verse 13: "So it shall be in that day: The great trumpet will be blown; They will come, who are about to perish in the land of Assyria, And they who are outcasts in the land of Egypt, And shall worship the Lord in the holy mount at Jerusalem."

The writer says that "in that day" the scattered would be gathered. This is the resurrection! (I will not document here that the ancient rabbis and the scholars clearly see this as a prophecy of the resurrection. See my book, *The Resurrection of Daniel 12:2: Fulfilled or Future?* for that documentation).

Notice, "in that day" is a direct reference to the time when the people that YHVH had created, the people of no understanding, would be judged, when the city and the temple would be destroyed! However, "in that day" the Lord would sound the Great Trumpet and gather those perishing in the lands of "exile"—that is the gathering of the dead!

57

As we have shown, Jesus was drawing from—directly echoing—Isaiah 27:13 in Matthew 24:31—"And He will send His angels with a great sound of a trumpet, and they will gather together His elect from the four winds, from one end of heaven to the other."

Now, since Jesus was drawing on Isaiah 27 in Matthew 24, this means that Jesus was predicting the resurrection. The parallels between Isaiah 27 and Matthew 24 are clear and undeniable:

O They both speak of the judgment of Jerusalem and the Temple.

O They both speak of the judgment on the disobedient people.

O They both speak of the gathering of the elect.

O They both speak of the gathering at the sound of the Trumpet.

O They both speak of the coming of the Lord at the time of the vindication of the martyrs (Isaiah 26:21/Matthew 23–24).

Now, unless one can show that either Isaiah 27 had nothing to do with Jesus' day and the events he was predicting,

or,

Unless it can be shown that Jesus was not echoing the prophecy of Isaiah and applying it to his coming,

or,

Unless it can be shown Isaiah's prophecy did not include the resurrection and the parallel constituent elements just listed are not truly parallel,

Then, it is more than evident that Isaiah's prophecy of the coming judgment of Jerusalem with the attendant destruction of the Temple was indeed a good news, bad news situation.

It was bad news because it was to be such a horrific judgment.

It was good news because it was to be the time of the salvation of the righteous remnant, the time of the resurrection, the time of salvation!

D. Daniel 12—I will not discuss Daniel 12 for space considerations, but, needless to say, that passage is determinative. It foretold the Great Tribulation (really *bad* news!). It foretold the resurrection (really *good* news!), the kingdom, the end of the age. And all of those things were to be fulfilled, "When the power of the holy people has been completely shattered" (Daniel 12:7).

The attempts by some former preterists to escape the force of Daniel 12 are literally astounding They are now inserting a 2500 year gap between Daniel 12:1 and verse 2—based strictly and solely on their literalistic and presuppositional insistence on a physical resurrection. It is amazing and amazingly sad to witness the theological gymnastics taking place! Be sure to get a copy of my book on Daniel 12 just mentioned for an in–depth discussion of that great chapter.

I think one can see that Jesus' prediction of the coming destruction of Jerusalem, as horrific as that was to be, was nonetheless, "this gospel of the kingdom" because of the blessings, the spiritual blessings that would become a reality at that time.

Answering Objection #2—Only Prophecies of Vengeance on Jerusalem were Fulfilled

In our examination of Jesus' statement that the announcement of the impending fall of Jerusalem was "the good news of the kingdom" (Matthew 24:14) I am asking the question of how that message of catastrophe could be called "the good news of the kingdom." How could an event and the events leading up to it, which Jesus described as the worst tribulation ever, be considered "good news" and especially the "good news of the *kingdom*"?

I just noted how the events of AD 70 would bring about the fulfillment of all things written (Luke 21:22). That alone was good news, because of the soteriological implications of the end of the Old Covenant age. But, there is more, much more reason for calling the end of the Old Covenant age "the gospel of the kingdom." Before developing more of those "good news" tenets, I am answering some objections to the claim that "all things written" were fulfilled. One of those objections, the second we are examining, is that AD 70 was "merely" the fulfillment of the prophecies of *the Day of Vengeance* on Israel.

Remember that when a person takes it upon themselves to "redefine" the meaning of words that it is their responsibility to prove that their definition is what is demanded by context. What I mean by that is that the objection that "all things written" in Luke 21:22 must refer only to "all things written concerning the fall of Jerusalem," or, in the case before us, "all things written concerning the Day of Vengeance against Jerusalem" must prove that the fall of Jerusalem had no significance beyond the fall of a city.[24] It must be shown also that the Days of

---

[24] It is now being claimed by some that the destruction of Jerusalem in AD 70 was not a covenantal judgment, i.e. the application of Mosaic Covenant sanctions found in Leviticus 26, Deuteronomy 28-30, and the fulfillment of Deuteronomy 32, the Song of Moses. Yet, John the Baptizer, as Elijah, was heralding the imminent coming of the Lord in judgment of Jerusalem for covenant violations (Malachi 3:1-6; 4:5-6). See my book, *Elijah has Come: A Solution to Romans 11:25-26*, for a full discussion. That book is available on my websites, Amazon, Kindle and other retailers. Simply stated, it is specious to deny that AD 70 was a covenantal judgment.

Vengeance were not in any way related to, inseparably tied to, the Day of Salvation,

The objection seeks to mitigate the force and application of "all things written." What is being affirmed, to express the objection another way, is that the fall of Jerusalem was a local judgment, not a "universal" judgment. So, the burden of proof demands that the objectors be able to prove that "all things written concerning the Day of Wrath" against Israel had no implications or application beyond Jerusalem of the first century. The Biblical reality is that while the "Wrath" was focused geographically on Judah and Jerusalem, that Day of Wrath was far, far more "extensive" than is normally granted. The implications of that Day of Wrath were not strictly "local" at all, as the objectors seek to say.[25]

It is interesting to me that even futurists often "slip up" and admit to the incredible meaning of AD 70. For instance, Thomas Ice, who I have debated, wrote the following, clearly not realizing the force of what he had said:

> Luke 21:20 must be A.D. 70 because it speaks of the days of vengeance, and this means "Those first century days are called 'days of vengeance' for Jerusalem is under the divine judgment of covenantal sanctions recorded in Leviticus 26 and Deuteronomy 28." Luke records that God's vengeance upon His elect nation is "in order that all things which are written may be fulfilled." Jesus is telling the

---

[25] See my series of articles on "The Great Day of God's Wrath and the End of the Millennium," on my website: www.donkpreston.com.

nation that God will fulfill all the curses of the Mosaic covenant because of Israel's disobedience. He will not relent and merely bring to pass a partial fulfillment of His vengeance. Some of the passages that Jesus said would be fulfilled include the following: Lev. 26:27–33; Deut. 28:49f; 32:19–27; 1 Kings 9:1–9; Jeremiah 6:1–8; 26:1–9;Daniel 9:26; Hosea 8:1–10; 10:15; Micah 3:12; Zechariah 11:6). (Thomas Ice, (Kenneth L. Gentry and Thomas Ice, *The Great Tribulation Past or Future?*, (Grand Rapids, MI; Kregel Publications, 1999), 98).

Do you catch the power of what Ice has admitted here? He is admitting that AD 70 was the fulfillment of "all the curses of the Mosaic Covenant." AD 70 was not a partial fulfillment of God's vengeance. It was the *total fulfillment!* Just take some time to examine the OT prophecies that Ice lists as fulfilled in AD 70, and consider the implications of his stunning admission. It is incredible. Although one could write a volume on the meaning of his admissions, I will refrain. I just wanted to take note that even some futurists point to the incredible significance of AD 70 as the fulfilling of God's wrath.

Now, as to the issue of the fulfillment of all things, consider the issue of the judgment of the nations. We are told that Matthew 25:31f must refer to an "end of time" scenario, because it speaks of all the nations being gathered for the great Assize. But, look a little closer, and particularly, look at what Jesus had to say about the judgment of the nations in Matthew 12:41–42:

"The men of Nineveh will rise up in the judgment with this generation and condemn it, because they repented at the preaching of Jonah; and indeed a greater than Jonah is here. 42 The queen of the South will rise up in the judgment with this generation and condemn it, for she came from the ends of the earth to hear the wisdom of Solomon; and indeed a greater than Solomon is here."

What do we have here? We have the judgment of Nineveh—a pagan city. We have the judgment of "the queen of the south"—another "pagan." And when would that be? At the judgment of Jerusalem/Israel of that generation!

In addition, consider Matthew 11:20–24:

> Then He began to rebuke the cities in which most of His mighty works had been done, because they did not repent: "Woe to you, Chorazin! Woe to you, Bethsaida! For if the mighty works which were done in you had been done in Tyre and Sidon, they would have repented long ago in sackcloth and ashes. But I say to you, it will be more tolerable for Tyre and Sidon in the day of judgment than for you. And you, Capernaum, who are exalted to heaven, will be brought down to Hades; for if the mighty works which were done in you had been done in Sodom, it would have remained until this day. But I say to you that it shall be more tolerable for the land of Sodom in the day of judgment than for you."

Now, Tyre and Sidon were pagan cities. They were truly "Gentile/pagan." And, surely no one would argue that *Sodom* was an Israelite city. There is simply no way to properly, truthfully consider these cities as "Israelite" cities. (There were no Jews or Israelites in the days of Sodom!). Only the most radical, presuppositional, desperate individuals would deny this or assert otherwise.

So, what is our point here? Follow along.

There is no question that the judgment of the nations is at the end of the age—in all futurist paradigms. That is beyond dispute. We are told that Matthew 25:31f is proof of this. And it is, when properly understood. Likewise, we are told that the judgment of the nations is the time when all prophecy would be fulfilled; all things written would be fulfilled.

Well, it is indisputably clear that the nations were to be judged at the end of the age—and that included the non–Jewish nations, even nations that extended centuries in the past from the first century! Nations that existed before there was even "Israel!"

In light of these facts, consider the following words of Jesus in Matthew 23:31–36:

> Therefore you are witnesses against yourselves that you are sons of those who murdered the prophets. Fill up, then, the measure of your fathers' guilt. Serpents, brood of vipers! How can you escape the condemnation of hell? Therefore, indeed, I send you prophets, wise men, and scribes: some of them you will kill and crucify, and some of them you will scourge in your synagogues and persecute from city to city, that on you may come all the righteous blood shed on the earth, from the blood of righteous Abel to the blood of Zechariah, son of Berechiah, whom you murdered between the temple and the altar. Assuredly, I say to you, all these things will come upon this generation.

Jesus said that Jerusalem would be judged in that generation. No one denies this. But, that is not the whole story. All of the blood, of all the righteous, *all the way back to Creation* would also be judged in that event. So, just how local was the judgment of Jerusalem? This text effectively negates the "argument" that is often given that the AD 70 judgment was too local to matter.

So, what we find then is that when Jesus said, "these be the days of vengeance in which all things that are written must be fulfilled" it is totally inappropriate to limit the extent of that fulfillment of Vengeance to Israel and Jerusalem. That vengeance spanned the time back to Creation. It encompassed the pagan nations! It truly was the fulfillment of all things written!

There is something else here that is extremely important, something I hinted at just briefly, and that is that Biblically, the Day of Vengeance/Wrath/Judgment was also the Day of Salvation. What this means is that to admit that the Day of Vengeance and Wrath was in AD 70, is to likewise admit that the Day of Salvation was at that time. This study alone would take up a great deal of space, so I will not develop it.[26]

Answering Objection #3—AD 70 Was the Fulfillment of Only Those Things That Had Been Written—i.e. the OT prophecies

Jesus said that the announcement of the coming destruction of Jerusalem and the kingdom was "this gospel of the kingdom." I have attempted to vindicate and explain how it was possible for Jesus to call that prediction of such a horrific event "the good news of the kingdom." One of the reasons that could be true is that it was in the events of the end of the Old Covenant age of Israel that all eschatological prophecy was fulfilled. Needless to say, that claim is rejected by any and all futurists who offer some objections to counter that claim.

I am answering the key objections to this claim. It is a claim by Dr. Kenneth Gentry, who has been an out–spoken critic of Covenant Eschatology. Gentry claims that "all things written" must refer strictly, solely and exclusively to all things written prior to when Jesus spoke

---

[26] For an extensive discussion, however, see my book, *Elijah Has Come: A Solution to Romans 11:25–27* (Ardmore, Ok; JaDon Management Inc., 2016). It is available on Amazon, Kindle, my websites and other retailers.

the words of Luke 21:22. In other words, for Gentry, "all things written" refers *only to the OT prophecies*. I will give here Gentry's argument and my response—edited and shortened—from my book, *AD 70: A Shadow of the "Real" End?*[27]

Gentry takes every opportunity to condemn preterists, but he refuses to actually engage in honorable discussions *with* preterists. He has been challenged *many* times by *numerous* people, including myself, to meet me in formal public debate. He invariably refuses.

As noted, Gentry clearly thinks he has found a fatal flaw in the preterist argument on Luke 21:22. Here is Gentry's argument:

In its context Luke 21:22 reads as follows: 'But when you see Jerusalem surrounded by armies, then recognize that her desolation is at hand. Then let those who are in Judea flee to the mountains and let those who are in the midst of the city depart and let not those who are in the country enter the city; because these are days of vengeance, in order that all things which are written may be fulfilled' (Lk 21:20–22).

Inarguably, (sic) the context here is focusing on AD 70, as even Dispensationalists agree.

The hyper–preterists naively assume that Jesus is speaking globally of absolutely all prophecies when he declares that 'all things which are written' will be fulfilled in AD 70. They hold, therefore, that no prophecy remains, which means that prophecies regarding the resurrection of all men, the second coming, and more came to pass in

---

[27] Don K. Preston, *Elijah Has Come*, (Ardmore, Ok; JaDon Management Inc., 2013). It is available on Amazon, Kindle, my websites and other retailers.

AD 70. They base their argument on deficient hermeneutics. Note just one deadly observation against their approach: The grammar of the passage limits the declaration. Jesus speaks of 'all things which are written' by employing a perfect passive participle: /gegrammena/ ('having been written'). This refers to prophecies already written—when he speaks in AD 30. Yet we know that more prophecies arise later in the New Testament revelation.

Once again we see a limitation on Jesus' statement. Furthermore, technically it does not even refer to any prophecy which Christ speaks. For these are not prophecies that have already been written. That being the case, the final resurrection (for instance) is outside of this declaration (Jn 5:28–29).

Thus, Jesus is referring to all things written in the Old Testament. At this stage of redemptive history those are the only prophecies that had already been written."[28]

Quite frankly, *I could hardly believe what I was reading* from the pen of the erudite Dr. Gentry. He has engaged in numerous debates. He surely knows one must be careful in making polemic arguments. The absolute desperation, the *total failure of logic* on the part of Dr. Gentry is glaring and egregious.

Let me summarize Dr. Gentry's argument for ease of understanding.

When Jesus said (Luke 21:22), that "all things written must be fulfilled," he referred only to those prophecies (and *all* of those prophecies), that had been written prior to his statement in AD 30.

---

[28]Kenneth Gentry, *He Shall Have Dominion: A Postmillennial Eschatology*, (Draper, VA; Apologetics Group Media, 2009), 542+.

All New Testament prophecies of the resurrection (e.g. John 5:28f, 1 Corinthians 15, 1 Thessalonians, etc.), were written after AD 30.

Therefore, all New Testament prophecies of the resurrection were not part of the "all things that are written" that were to be fulfilled in the fall of Jerusalem in AD 70.

Here is what Dr. Gentry concludes: "Thus, Jesus is referring to all things written in the Old Testament. At this stage of redemptive history those are the only prophecies that had already been written."

Gentry's "logic," if such it can be called, fails on a number of points. However, I will only make two points in response to his amazing argument.

Argument #1—The New Testament prophecies of the resurrection are simply the reiteration of the Old Testament prophecies *(things already written in A.D. 30)*.

Proof of this argument: I need only refer to the words of Paul. The apostle affirmed in the most unambiguous manner that his doctrine of the resurrection was *nothing* but what was found in the Old Testament, i.e. *in that which had already been written*!

Acts 24:14–15: "But this I confess to you, that according to the Way which they call a sect, so I worship the God of my fathers, believing all things which are written in the Law and in the Prophets. I have hope in God, which they themselves also accept, that there will be a resurrection of the dead, both of the just and the unjust."

Paul said his doctrine of the resurrection of the dead, for which he was on trial, was found in Moses and the Law and the prophets. That certainly qualifies as that which was written before A.D. 30.

Acts 26:21–23: "Having therefore obtained help of God, I continue unto this day, witnessing both to small and great, saying none other things than those which the prophets and Moses did say should come: That Christ should suffer, and that he should be the first that should rise from the dead, and should shew light unto the people, and to the Gentiles."

Paul said he preached nothing, *nothing* but the hope of Israel found in Moses and the prophets. *Do you catch the power of that?*

Paul taught of the resurrection of the dead.

But, Paul did not preach anything but the hope of Israel found in Moses and the prophets.

Therefore, the doctrine of the resurrection of the dead was found in Moses and the prophets.

Romans 8:23; 9:1–4: "And not only they, but ourselves also, which have the first fruits of the Spirit, even we ourselves groan within ourselves, waiting for the *adoption*, to wit, the redemption of our body...For I could wish that myself were accursed from Christ for my brethren, my kinsmen according to the flesh: Who are Israelites; *to whom pertaineth the adoption*, and the glory, and the covenants, and the giving of the law, and the service of God, and the promises."

The adoption, according to Paul, was the resurrection.

But, the promise of the adoption was given to, and belonged to, Israel after the flesh.

This means the adoption, the promise of the resurrection, was from the Old Testament prophecies.

69

1 Corinthians 15:54–55: "So when this corruptible shall have put on incorruption, and this mortal shall have put on immortality, then shall be brought to pass the saying that is written, Death is swallowed up in victory. O death, where is thy sting? O grave, where is thy victory?" Paul cites Isaiah 25:8 and Hosea 13:14 as the source of his resurrection doctrine in Corinthians.

Paul said the resurrection would be when Isaiah 25 and Hosea 13:14 would be fulfilled.

Thus, the resurrection hope and doctrine of 1 Corinthians 15 was found in, and based on the Old Testament prophecies made to Israel.

From these texts, it is undeniable that the resurrection hope expressed by the New Testament writers was nothing other than a reiteration of what had already been written long ago in the Old Testament scriptures! This is *fatal* to Gentry's argument and theology.

It is simply wrong to say the New Testament prophecies of the resurrection are not grounded in and based on the Old Covenant prophecies. This is to deny Paul who said he preached nothing but the hope of Israel found in Moses and the prophets. 1 Corinthians 15 is not different from Isaiah 25 or Hosea 13:14, for Paul says that when the resurrection occurred, it would be the fulfillment of those prophecies. To say 1 Corinthians 15 is the explication of those prophecies is not the same as saying they are different from those prophecies.

Therefore, you cannot say all Old Testament prophecies were fulfilled at the AD 70 parousia of Christ, without affirming the fulfillment of all New Testament eschatology. There is no "new" eschatology in the New Testament. *All New Testament eschatology is the anticipation of the imminent fulfillment of Old Testament promises.* Period. This totally falsifies Gentry's specious argument.

Argument #2—For argument sake therefore, I will most gladly accept Dr. Gentry's own summary statement: "Thus, Jesus is referring to *all things written in the Old Testament*. At this stage of redemptive history those are the only prophecies that had already been written." (My emphasis, DKP)

Consider then the following argument:

All things written in the Old Testament, i.e. all Old Testament prophecy, was fulfilled by the time of, and in the events of, the fall of Jerusalem in AD 70. (Gentry).

But, the Old Testament prophesied of the resurrection of the dead (Acts 24:14f; 26:6f; 26:21f, Romans 8:23; 9:1–4, 1 Corinthians 15:54–55).

Therefore, the prophecies of the resurrection of the dead were fulfilled by the time of, and in the events of, the fall of Jerusalem in AD 70.

This argument is *prima facie* true.

It is *incontrovertibly true* that the Old Testament foretold the resurrection of the dead. Gentry agrees.

It is *irrefutably true* that all New Testament prophecies of the resurrection are drawn from and the reiteration of the Old Testament prophecies.

It is *undeniable* that Jesus said all things written would be fulfilled bythe time of, and in the events of the fall of Jerusalem in A.D. 70.

Gentry is correct in affirming that *all Old Testament prophecies* would be fulfilled at/in AD 70. And this proves, *beyond refutation*, that the resurrection of the dead came at the dissolution of the Old Covenant age of Israel in AD 70.[29]

Incidentally, it would do no good for Gentry, or anyone else, to amend his statement and argue that all Jesus really meant was that all Old Covenant prophecies *concerning the fall of Jerusalem* were to be fulfilled in AD 70. (Note that Gentry made no attempt to limit the scope of the Old Covenant prophecies to be fulfilled in AD 70. He said emphatically, "Jesus is referring to *all things written in the Old Testament*").

The indisputable fact is that in the Old Testament the resurrection of the dead is *repeatedly* posited at the destruction of Old Covenant Israel. Note a couple of examples.

---

[29] See my presentation on "The Preterist Perspective of the Millennium" presented at Criswell College, Dallas, Texas, in October of 2012 demonstrating how the OT not only foretold the end of the millennium resurrection, but, repeatedly posited it at the time of the avenging of the blood of the martyrs. Jesus' teaching in Matthew 23 definitively posits that as AD 70. Also, in my formal debate with Joel McDurmon, my main point was proving that the OT posited the end of the millennium resurrection at the end of Israel's covenant age. The Criswell CD is available from me. DVDs and a book of the McDurmon debate are available from my websites).

Isaiah 25:1–8 —

O LORD, You are my God. I will exalt You, I will praise Your name, For You have done wonderful things; Your counsels of old are faithfulness and truth. 2 For You have made a city a ruin, A fortified city a ruin, A palace of foreigners to be a city no more; It will never be rebuilt. Therefore the strong people will glorify You; The city of the terrible nations will fear You. For You have been a strength to the poor, A strength to the needy in his distress, A refuge from the storm, A shade from the heat; For the blast of the terrible ones is as a storm against the wall. You will reduce the noise of aliens, As heat in a dry place; As heat in the shadow of a cloud, The song of the terrible ones will be diminished. And in this mountain The LORD of hosts will make for all people A feast of choice pieces, A feast of wines on the lees, Of fat things full of marrow, Of well–refined wines on the lees. And He will destroy on this mountain The surface of the covering cast over all people, And the veil that is spread over all nations. He will swallow up death forever, And the Lord GOD will wipe away tears from all faces; The rebuke of His people He will take away from all the earth; For the LORD has spoken.

Note that in the day that YHVH would destroy death, it would also be when He made the city a desolation and turned the temple over to foreigners. The city under consideration is the "city of confusion" in chapter 24:10f, Ariel, i.e. Jerusalem. So, Isaiah emphatically posits the resurrection at the time of Jerusalem's demise.

In chapter 26:19–21, the Lord predicted the resurrection at the time when YHVH would come out of heaven and avenge the blood of the martyrs. Of course, Jesus was emphatically clear that all of the righteous blood of all the saints, shed on the earth, would be avenged in the judgment of Jerusalem in A.D. 70 (Matthew 23:34f).

In Isaiah 27:1f, we find the destruction of Leviathan, the enemy of God, defeated in the day of the Lord's coming. This is the Day of 26:19f, i.e. the day of the resurrection. And, this Day of the Lord would also be when the people YHVH had created would no longer receive mercy. He would turn the altar to chalk stones (Isaiah 27:9f). Thus, again, the resurrection is clearly placed in the context of the judgment of Jerusalem and Israel.

There are in fact several OT passages which posit the resurrection in the context of the judgment of Israel. It is of interest to me that other than Daniel 12 on which he has changed his views, I have found little comment from Gentry about the OT predictions of the resurrection. In his massive tome of 2009, he does not mention Isaiah 25–27 or Hosea, even though Paul cited these verses as the source of his resurrection doctrine in 1 Corinthians 15:54f. (Interestingly, Gentry does comment on Isaiah 26 as the final resurrection in his 1992 version of *Dominion* (p. 283, 284).

The point of course is that it will do Gentry no good whatsoever to now say that all Jesus really meant to say was, "these be the days of vengeance in which all things that are written about the fall of Jerusalem will be fulfilled." On one level, we could agree with this, for as it has been demonstrated, the fall of Jerusalem was in fact to be the time of the resurrection.

Gentry has, *through his own argument*, destroyed his Postmillennial, futurist eschatology. He has actually confirmed the truthfulness of "hyper–preterism!" And along the way, he has falsified the claim that the events of AD 70 were typological of another resurrection. If all OT prophecies have been fulfilled, then since the OT predicted the final, end of the millennium resurrection, clearly, the fulfillment of those eschatological prophecies was not typological of anything else in our future.

All of this means that all eschatological prophecies have been fulfilled. That is "the good news of the kingdom!" It is good news for all those who believe in Jesus!

Answering Objection #4—All things Were fulfilled at the Cross When Jesus Said "It is finished"—John 19:30

I have and do affirm that the time of the fall of Jerusalem was the time when "all things written" were fulfilled. God's eschatological and soteriological schema was completed, the unending New Covenant age of Messiah came fully into play.

This is an examination of the fourth objection to that claim to be examined. The objection maintains that when Jesus was still on the cross and he said, "It is finished" that this was indicating that the Old Law, the Law of Moses, was now completed. That is the time, we are told, when the Law of Moses was nailed to the cross. While this is a common belief, and one that I personally espoused for many years, I do not believe it is Biblical.

So, what then did Jesus mean when he cried out, "It is finished"? We need to understand a bit about *prolepsis* to understand John 19.

75

Prolepsis is speaking of something as if it is finished, when in reality it is so sure to be finished, or is so close to being finished, that it is spoken of as a completed reality.

Consider John 17:4, where Jesus, before the cross, said, "I have finished the work which You have given me to do." Jesus had clearly not yet finished that work, he had not even died yet.

Was Jesus wrong in John 17? Did he lie? No, patently not. He spoke as if the work was finished knowing that the sacrificial work was about to be finished. And yet, the full outworking of the Atonement was not yet completed, as Hebrews 9 shows.

The claim that Jesus's cry, "It is finished" (John 19:30) meant that he was signifying that the Law itself was now finished is an unfortunate and ill–informed claim. It completely overlooks the place of the fulfillment of Israel's feast days in God's scheme. Consider the following:

Passover—which is when Jesus was crucified—was the first of Israel's feast days (See Exodus 12–14). It initiated the first four feast days, the feast of Unleavened Bread, the Feast of Weeks and Pentecost (or First–Fruit). Pentecost was the last of those first four festivals.

Keep in mind that Israel's New Moons, Feast Days and Sabbaths were shadows of the better things that were to come (Colossians 2:14f). When Paul wrote Colossians, years after the Cross, he was still anticipating the fulfillment of those types and shadows. He set forth Jesus as the "body" i.e. the reality that the Old Covenant shadows pointed to. It is essential to honor the present active indicatives in the text when he says that those Sabbatical feast days "are" (his present tense situation) a shadow of the good things "about to come." So, for

76

Paul, Israel's festal calendar was not yet fulfilled. But, one thing is certain, fulfillment had begun!

Paul called attention to the fact that Jesus was the Passover sacrifice (1 Corinthians 5). His death on the Cross was the "reality" to which the original Passover pointed. But, ask yourself the question: Was Israel's festal calendar finished/consummated/finalized with the completion of the Passover sacrifice—the first of the seven feast days? Patently not. What then is the meaning of, "It is finished"? As we will see momentarily, it meant that just as the High Priest was declaring that the typological Passover ceremony was finished, Jesus, the True High Priest, was declaring that the True Passover sacrifice was completed. With the Passover sacrifice offered, the other feast days were about to be finished. It actually meant that the festal calendar was now underway—not that it was finished! To get a bit of better understanding and appreciation for the Passover, and even its eschatological role, we need to look at history for corroboration and understanding of Jesus' cry: "It is finished" as it related to the Passover. We can look to both the Passover meal, and to the Temple actions during Passover to appreciate what Jesus said as he was on the Cross. I will share below from an earlier article that I did, with some editing.

In regard to the preliminary Passover meal and its typological significance, Pitre has some insightful comments. He speaks of the four cups of Passover. The fourth cup was the final cup to conclude the Passover.

Jesus did not initially take the fourth cup. He said, "I will not drink of this fruit of the vine, until I take it in my father's kingdom." In other words, *Jesus did not finish the Passover!* However, Pitre then shows how in the Garden, Jesus said "let this cup pass from me."

Pitre then shows how on the Cross, Jesus initially refused the wine mixed with gall (Matthew 27:31–36), which was given to those about to die to kill the pain, but, he then requested a drink. They gave him sour wine on a sponge, and that is when Jesus said, "It is finished."

Pitre notes, "When Jesus said, 'It is finished,' he was not referring to his life or his messianic mission. For he did not say it until his request for a drink had been answered. He did not say it until 'he had received the wine.' Why? What does that mean? Once again, when we remember Jesus' vow at the Last Supper, and his prayer about drinking the 'cup' in Gethsemane, then the meaning of Jesus' last word becomes clear. It means that *Jesus did in fact drink the fourth cup of the Jewish Passover*. It means that he did in fact finish the Last Supper. But, he did not do it in the Upper Room. He did it on the cross. He did it at the very moment of his death." (Brant Pitre, *Jesus and the Jewish Roots of the Eucharist*. New York: Doubleday; 2011, 155f).

An examination of the cups of Passover and how the NT writers utilized the typology of the Supper is helpful and full of meaning.

1. Festival Blessing—Drink from 1st cup of wine.

2. Passover Narrative and Little Hallel (Psalm 113)—Drink from 2nd cup of wine.

3. Main Meal: Eat the roasted lamb, unleavened bread, and the bitter herbs and spices. *This third cup was called the Cup of Blessing.* Note then 1 Corinthians 11:16f where Paul said, "The Cup of Blessing which we bless, is it not the communion of the blood of Christ?"

This is highly suggestive. The third cup, in Jewish thought, signified salvation through suffering: The third cup was drunk in connection with Exodus 6:6c: "I will also redeem you with an outstretched arm and with great judgments." Thus, it symbolized redemption by judgment. (Brant Pitre, *Jesus and the Jewish Roots of the Eucharist.* New York: Doubleday, 2011; 147f).

So, when Paul spoke of the Supper and the "Cup of Blessing" in direct connection with the suffering of Christ, does this not suggest that the fourth cup—like Jesus did—would be taken with the filling up of the measure of suffering? Just as Jesus drank the fourth cup on the cross, i.e. through finishing his sacrifice, the early church had to drink the fourth cup by filling up the measure of suffering that Jesus foretold in Matthew 23:29f.

Thus, in 1 Corinthians 11:26 when Paul spoke of, "shewing forth the Lord's death until he comes" he was referring to their participation in Christ's suffering and the consequent impending consummation of the last days, eschatological suffering of the early church as they participated in "the sufferings of Christ" (Cf. Romans 8:17) and anticipated "the glory" about to be revealed (2 Thessalonians 1:10f; 1 Peter 5:1f, etc.).

4. The Passover is completed with the singing of the Great Hallel (PSALMS 114–118), the drinking of the 4th cup of wine, and closed when the presiding priest or host says the phrase, "TEL TELESTE" which is interpreted as "IT IS FINISHED" or "IT IS CONSUMMATED".[30]

Failure to integrate the typology of the Passover meal and the cups into our interpretation of several NT passages surely leads to a failure to fully appreciate what the writers were saying. The richness of this

---

[30]https://www.chabad.org/holidays/passover/pesach_ cdo/aid/658520/jewish/What-is-the-significance-of-the-four-cups.htm.

kind of study can hardly be over–emphasized. Unfortunately, the significance of Israel's festal calendar for understanding the NT is greatly ignored or overlooked.

In regard to the Temple practice of the Passover, it is incredible to consider what was taking place in the Temple *at the very moment Jesus—the True Passover—was on the Cross.* Consider the following material.

IT IS FINISHED (John 19:30)
At Passover, the lamb that the high priest chose was staked at the temple mount for the public to inspect. All could inspect it for four days before it was offered up for sacrifice. The thousands of lambs would then be sacrificed, starting at around 9:00 am. The shofar would sound to announce to the surrounding areas that the last lamb of about 250,000 (over 40,000 per hour) had been slaughtered. This would be about 3:00 pm. The blood from the slaughter was in such volume that it shone in the brazen pans as the sunlight reflected on it. This red glow (shine) was evident from the hills a long distance away. The High Priest who had closely inspected the lamb, satisfied it was unblemished (perfect), would say: "I find no fault in him" (John 18:38, 19:4,6). The main lamb offering at the temple mount during Passover was made by the High Priest after all the others had been made, about 3:00 pm. Starting at about 9:00 am the High priest was required (by tradition) to stand there for about six hours and supervise until all the lambs were sacrificed. It was exactly six hours that Yeshua hung on the stake before He died. After the High Priest offered up the last lamb the High priest would say "I thirst". He would then wet his lips with water

and proclaim that "it is finished", meaning the slaughtering of all the lambs for Passover. It was exactly 3:00 pm when Yeshua gave up His Spirit and said His last words; "It is finished." If you recall, as part of the Jewish wedding tradition the father of the groom to be would declare to his son "it is finished", when the groom's house was complete. He was then able to go get his bride. Does this sound familiar?

Yeshua too was the last lamb sacrificed and He would have heard the sound of the shofar blasting as He gave up His life for us. Yeshua wasn't killed for us, He died for us (Luke 23:44–45). "It was now about the sixth hour, and darkness fell over the whole land until the ninth hour, because the sun was obscured; and the veil of the temple was torn in two."

Just so you can get a good idea of how strong the Temple veil was, keep this in mind. When testing the second veil in front of the Holy of Holies in the Temple, two pair of oxen were attached to either end of the veil. If the oxen could split the veil, it was not made strong enough. Luke 23 was the fulfillment of Isa. 50:3 "I clothe the heavens with blackness And make sackcloth their covering."

John 19:30 Therefore when Yeshua had received the sour wine, He said, "It is finished!" And He bowed His head and gave up His spirit. The analogy is so beautiful. The more we learn about the Feasts, the more analogies we see between Yeshua and everything associated with Him in the Scriptures.

(EOQ. see also Ps.22:31).[31]

The point of all of this is to show—very powerfully—that when Jesus cried out, "It is finished!" that he was by no means declaring that the Law of Moses was finished. He was declaring that his suffering *as the Passover Lamb* was finished. But, when viewed through the prism of the Jewish Festal Calendar, what that meant was that God was now in the process of bringing the types and shadows of the entire calender to fulfillment. And we see that in the resurrection of Jesus and in the events of Pentecost, the last of the first four feast days.

In light of all of this, there is no justification whatsoever for claiming that the Law of Moses would pass away with the fulfillment of only one—the first one—of God's feast days—all of which were types and shadows. Jesus' words "It is finished" simply conveyed the idea that Passover—his sacrificial suffering—was now finished.

So, John 19:30 does not prove that all things necessary were fulfilled. Essentially, that text shows us that the initial festal calendar was fulfilled. But, that meant that the countdown to the end, the fulfillment of the final three feast days, was not far off. And it would be then—at the fulfillment of Rosh Hashanah, Yom Kippur and Succot that all things written would finally be fulfilled. When those typological, foreshadowing—eschatological—feast days were fulfilled, the full application of God's promises of salvation would become a reality and in the fulfillment of those final feast days, is to be found the greatest news of all!

---

[31] Found at: http://messianicgentiles.blogspot.com/ 2009/11/it-is-finished-john-1930.html (at time of publication this link had been removed.)

How Could Jesus Call the Message of the Impending Fall of Jerusalem, the Gospel (the "Good News!") of the Kingdom?

Point # 7

The Fall of Jerusalem was The End of the Age of Shadows and Types—The Reality Came!

When asking and seeking answers to the question of how the message of the fall of Jerusalem could have been—or could be today—called "this Gospel of the Kingdom" it is critical to realize that Israel and the Old Covenant praxis (Sabbath, Circumcision, Temple, priesthood, etc.) that identified her, set her apart from the nations, was *typological*. Those things foreshadowed the "better things to come," as Paul expressed it in Colossians 2. (And don't forget that Paul said those better things were foreshadowed by the New Moons, feast days and Sabbaths, were "about to come"). That means that the shadow form of Israel was about to pass because what the types pointed to was about to become a reality.

But look again at this: the arrival of the "body," the reality, meant *the passing away of the shadow*, the type. This answers the question posed just above: How could Jesus' statement that the impending destruction of the Temple and Jerusalem was to be proclaimed as "gospel" i.e. good news, indeed, the "good news of the kingdom"? After all, that horrific catastrophe was described by Jesus himself as the worst tribulation in the history of the world—the worst that would ever be? So, again, how was that, how could that be, *good news*?

The answer is to be found in the fact that the Old Covenant Temple, as well as the Old Covenant city of Jerusalem, was a type of the better, the heavenly, the "real" Temple of God. Simply stated, the passing of the Old could be "good news" because that passing meant that the "Real," the "True," was being established.

Notice Hebrews 8:1–2:

> Now this is the main point of the things we are
> saying: We have such a High Priest, who is seated at
> the right hand of the throne of the Majesty in the
> heavens, a Minister of the sanctuary and of the true
> tabernacle which the Lord erected, and not man.

Did you catch it? The New Covenant Temple/Tabernacle that was
established by Christ, which is unequivocally *the church of the living
God* (1 Corinthians 3:16; 2 Corinthians 6:14–16; Ephesians 2:19f,
etc.) is called the *"True Tabernacle."* Let me give again Beale's
comments on Hebrews 8:1f:

> Hebrews refers to the heavenly tabernacle as 'true'
> because it is the fulfillment, not only of direct
> prophecies of the eschatological temple, but, of
> everything the Old Testament tabernacle and temples
> foreshadowed (2004, 296).

Likewise, Lane says the use of "true": "Implies genuine, of effective
value, and the expression 'true tabernacle' is used in contrast not to
what is false, but to what is symbolical and imperfect."[32]

The fact that the Old Covenant Temple pointed to something else,
something better, the "real" Temple of God, is shown in Hebrews
9:23–24:

---

[32] William Lane, *Word Biblical Commentary,
Hebrews 1–8, 47a*, (Dallas; Word, 1991), 205+.

85

Therefore it was necessary that the copies of the things in the heavens should be purified with these, but the heavenly things themselves with better sacrifices than these. For Christ has not entered the holy places made with hands, which are copies of the true, but into heaven itself, now to appear in the presence of God for us.

Here, the writer sets before his audience that the heavenly Temple is the real one, and that it was what the earthy temple, "made with hands" looked forward to, foreshadowed.

Notice also that the text says that the heavenly temple was "better." It was sanctified by "better sacrifices" (i.e the sacrifice of Jesus) than the Old Covenant Temple. There are two things that should impress us here.

Even in the Tanakh, we find the recognition that the earthly Temple, no matter how magnificent it might be, was totally insufficient to hold the Presence of YHVH. When he dedicated the wonderful Temple he had built, Solomon acknowledged this fact: "But will God indeed dwell on the earth? Behold, heaven and the heaven of heavens cannot contain You. How much less this temple which I have built!" (1 Kings 8:27).

At a later period, after the destruction of that temple, Israel longed for the restoration of that glory. Yet, God warned them to not place too much emphasis on a physical edifice, and to look to Him: Thus says the Lord:

"Heaven is My throne, And earth is My footstool. Where is the house that you will build Me? And where is the place of My rest? For all those things My

86

hand has made, And all those things exist," says the Lord. "But on this one will I look: On him who is poor and of a contrite spirit, And who trembles at My word" (Isaiah 66:1–2).

It is important to see that this text emphasized the importance of the heart (faith) as the criteria for the Presence of YHVH. Then, the text goes ahead to predict the coming destruction of the Old Covenant City—and the Temple that would reside there (Isaiah 66:2–6):

> Thus Says the Lord.: "But on this one will I look: On him who is poor and of a contrite spirit, And who trembles at My word. He who kills a bull is as if he slays a man; He who sacrifices a lamb, as if he breaks a dog's neck; He who offers a grain offering, as if he offers swine's blood; He who burns incense, as if he blesses an idol. Just as they have chosen their own ways, And their soul delights in their abominations, So will I choose their delusions, And bring their fears on them; Because, when I called, no one answered, When I spoke they did not hear; But they did evil before My eyes, And chose that in which I do not delight." Hear the word of the Lord, You who tremble at His word: "Your brethren who hated you, Who cast you out for My name's sake, said, 'Let the Lord be glorified, That we may see your joy.' But they shall be ashamed." The sound of noise from the city! *A voice from the temple!* The voice of the Lord, Who fully repays His enemies! (My emphasis, DKP).

So, we have here a declaration by YHVH that the Old Covenant Temple was insufficient. It was not glorious enough. He likewise castigated Israel for refusing to hear Him (and Paul cites this verse and

Isaiah 65:1–2) as being fulfilled in his day. We then find the prediction of a coming desolation of the city and the temple in the Day of the Lord. This is incredible!

With all due respect, I believe that every Dispensationalist should ponder these words carefully. I will not develop it here but, it is important to see that Isaiah 66 falsifies the Dispensational postponement doctrine. (Be sure to read my series of articles on Isaiah 66 that can be found on my website: www.donkpreston.com). In the text, YHVH was predicting the coming of the Lord for both the salvation and the judgment of Israel. He foretold the New Creation. And notice that in v. 9, the Lord said: "Shall I bring to the time of birth, and not bring forth?" This "birth" is clearly the kingdom following the "birth pains of Messiah." YHVH was asserting that He would not fail. He would not postpone. He would not only bring Israel to the time of birth, He would bring forth his purpose—the kingdom! This is fatal to Dispensationalism.

Essentially from the beginning, YHVH told Israel that physical temples were not what He wanted. They could not hold Him. How could it be possible that YHVH wants to one day rebuild a temple when He constantly emphasized how insufficient any physical edifice was, and how, in contrast, He desires to dwell with those of faith? He told them that the Old Covenant Temple pointed to something else, something "better" than the glorious Temples constructed in Jerusalem.

So, given the indisputable fact that the New Testament teaches us that the church of the living God is the True Temple to which the Old Temple looked, why in the world would anyone look with eager expectation to the rebuilding of a physical temple in Jerusalem? Physical temples can never be the True Temple of God! And neither can the literal city of Jerusalem. It cannot be the True City of God

88

because it always—always—pointed to the True City of God, the "heavenly Jerusalem."

Herein lies the answer to our question that we posed earlier in regard to the fact that Jesus said the prediction of the impending destruction of Jerusalem and the Temple: How could Jesus call the impending destruction of Jerusalem and the Temple the "good news of the kingdom" (Matthew 24:14)? He could call it "this gospel (good news) of the kingdom." He could do so because the removal of the Old Covenant Temple and City meant that the long–anticipated New Covenant and City would be fully realized with the demise of the Old.

It would also be good news to his followers, because while the rulers of the Old Covenant world would become "the enemies of the Cross" (1 Corinthians 2:6f; Philippians 3:16–18) and cause a world–wide persecution against the followers of Jesus, with the destruction of Jerusalem and the Temple, the organized persecution of the saints was shattered. Good news indeed.

Once the Dispensational world realizes and accepts the typological and shadow nature of Israel and her world, Dispensationalism itself falls to the ground. Christ and the gospel world is—as we have shown—what Israel and her world pointed to. We have proven, from Scripture, that even Dispensationalists (unwittingly) agree that the Old Covenant did in fact predict the establishment of the church and the Gospel as the New Covenant. So, when Christ, the mediator of the New Covenant arrived, the Old Covenant world was supposed to pass away—yes, be replaced—with the everlasting Gospel of Christ. Look again at the list of the types and shadows of the Old Covenant world of Israel.

V The Old Covenant itself was *supposed* to be "replaced" by the New Covenant (Jeremiah 31; Hebrews 8).

V The Old Covenant land was *supposed* to be "replaced" by the heavenly "father land" (Hebrews 11).

V The Old Covenant City was *supposed* to be "replaced" by the "heavenly Jerusalem" the city of the Living God (Hebrews 12:21f).

V The Old Covenant physical circumcision was *supposed* to be "replaced" by the circumcision of the heart. (Romans 2:28f; Philippians 3:1–5, etc.). The subject of circumcision is troubling for the Dispensational world. It is an issue that they simply do not like to discuss since under the Gospel, physical circumcision is forbidden. Yet, Dispensationalism posits the restoration of that mandate. This demands that in the proposed future kingdom, a believer in Christ has the choice: be circumcised and forfeit Christ's grace, or, refuse to be circumcised, and incur God's wrath! There is no way to harmonize the Dispensational view of the kingdom and the doctrine of physical circumcision.

V The Old Covenant genealogically restricted priesthood was *supposed* to be "replaced" by the nation of priests, "he has made us to be a kingdom of priests" (Revelation 1:5f).

V The Old Covenant, ineffective animal sacrifices were *supposed* to be "replaced" by the perfect, one time for all time, sacrifice of Jesus (Hebrews 10:5f). It is more than baffling and disturbing to realize that there are those who now posit a return to Torah keeping. This includes animal sacrifices. The writer of Hebrews says that YHVH never had pleasure in animal sacrifices and they could never take away sin. He added that once forgiveness was actualized, "there is no more offering for sin" (Hebrews 10:5f). Thus, when it is insisted that Torah be observed, with its animal sacrifices, this is tantamount to saying that there is no forgiveness of sin today. The Dispensational posit of animal sacrifices in the proposed millennium is equally disturbing.

V The Old Covenant physical Temple was *supposed* to be "replaced" by the True Tabernacle that God pitched, and not man (Hebrews 8:1–2).

V The Old Covenant physical people was *supposed* to be "replaced" by the people yet to be created (Psalms 102; Isaiah 43; Isaiah 65, etc.).[33]

All of this was God's plan from the very beginning. Thus, to reiterate, Replacement Theology is as Biblical as it can be. Not in the sense that God ripped Israel's promises from her and gave them to someone else, as posited by Amillennialists and Postmillennialists. No, that is a false doctrine. As Paul affirmed in Romans 11, YHVH was faithful to those Old Covenant promises. This is *replacement through fulfillment*. The Dispensationalists must come to grips with a proper understanding of Romans 11:25–27.[34]

---

[33] For a full discussion of the issue of Replacement Theology get a copy of my book, *One Root, One Kingdom— All Nations!* (Ardmore, Ok; JaDon Management Inc., 2017). Available on Amazon, Kindle and my websites). While it is surely wrong to speak of the replacement of Old Covenant Israel, based on the premise of her *failure*, it is Biblically sound, solid and sure, that God originally intended for Israel's distinctive role to be temporary. When she had accomplished her purpose, to bring the Messiah to the world, that salvation, which was "to the Jew first" would then flow to the nations.

[34] See my book, *Elijah Has Come: A Solution to Romans 11:25-27*, for an in-depth examination of Romans 11 and the ministry of John the Baptizer. It is my contention that when we correlate John's ministry and message with Romans 11, that it demands a first–century fulfillment of Paul's

That is that God's faithfulness to Old Covenant Israel always included the termination of the Old Covenant world. The end of the shadows, the fulfillment of the types, demanded that the limited, exclusivistic nation give way to the long–promised people that would include all men, any person. We will not go into further detail on that, since I think we have established it beyond dispute.

But, someone may say that while it may be true that the land, the city, the temple, etc. were all types and shadows of the coming better things (which is a fatal admission when properly considered) but, that does not prove that Israel herself was a type or shadow of another people, a new people.

We should not miss the connection between the message of the coming dissolution of the Temple and the "kingdom" message: "This *gospel* of the *kingdom* must be preached..." What this means is that while far too many "commentators" deride the significance of the destruction of the City and Temple as merely a local judgment with virtually no spiritual significance, to Jesus, there is a direct, inseparable connection between that cataclysmic event and the *kingdom*.

In Luke 21:28–32, the connection is clear: the New Covenant Kingdom of heaven would come in power and glory—in its full manifestation—at the passing of the Old Covenant Kingdom! See Isaiah 65:8–19. That is the best news possible!

---

promise of the salvation of Israel at the coming of the Lord. The book is available on Amazon, Kindle, my websites and other retailers.

How Could Jesus Call the Message of the Impending Fall of Jerusalem, the Gospel (the "Good News!") of the Kingdom?

Point # 8

It Was When Man Could Enter the Most Holy Place and Receive Salvation!
The End of the Ministration of Death

As I suggested above, the end of the Old Covenant age in AD 70 was the time when the types and shadows of the Old Covenant were fulfilled. Understanding the centrality of Israel's cultic world—centered in the Temple—comes into play here.

Jerusalem was considered the center of the world (Ezekiel 5:8f). The Temple was the center of the center of Israel's entire world. The Jews believed in ten concentric circles of holiness.[35]

The Most Holy Place was the center of the center of the world. Josephus informs us that in Jewish thought, the Holy Place was called "earth" because that is where the priests, representing man, functioned. The Most Holy was called "heaven" because it was the dwelling place of God Himself (Josephus, *Antiquities*, 6:3:4). That inner court was sacrosanct, inviolable. Standing between the Holy Place and the Most Holy was the marvelous veil. This veil represented the natural creation with its four main colors, but, it also stood as a constant symbol of the separation between God and man.

---

[35]https://www.sefaria.org/Mishnah_Kelim.1?lang=bi

As Josephus indicated, and as Jewish authorities and countless scholars have noted, the MHP represented the very presence of God. Because of the inability of the Old Covenant cultus to remove sin— "the blood of bulls and goats can never take away sin"—(Hebrews 10:1–3) no one was allowed into that sacred place except the High Priest on Yom Kippur, the Day of Atonement. No matter how many sacrifices were offered, they did not provide objective "real time", to use a modern term, forgiveness. In fact, in those sacrifices "there was a remembrance of sin" every year (Hebrews 10:1–4). Not forgiveness—*remembrance of sin*!

Consider in light of all of this, Hebrews 9:6–10:

> Now when these things had been thus prepared, the priests always went into the first part of the tabernacle, performing the services. But into the second part the high priest went alone once a year, not without blood, which he offered for himself and for the people's sins committed in ignorance; the Holy Spirit indicating this, that the way into the Holiest of All was not yet made manifest while the first tabernacle was still standing. It was symbolic for the present time in which both gifts and sacrifices are offered which cannot make him who performed the service perfect in regard to the conscience— concerned only with foods and drinks, various washings, and fleshly ordinances imposed until the time of reformation.

Here, the inspired writer makes it clear that due to the insufficiency and weakness of the animal sacrifices and cultic praxis to take away sin, that man could not enter the MHP. As long as that system was "imposed" (from *epikeimena*, ἐπικείμενα Strong's #1945) having *standing* (v. 8, from *stasin*, στάσιν Strong's #4714—this does not mean the simple physical edifice still "standing" but, having standing, i.e. validity) there could be no entrance into the MHP.

Now, the majority of evangelical Christianity claims that the Law of Moses, with its cultus, was "nailed to the cross." Appeal is made to Colossians 2:14f. Unfortunately for that view, that text does not prove the case, but just the opposite. I will not discuss that here, but, see my book *The Passing of the Law: Torah To Telos* for a full discussion.

To put our case as simply as possible:

As long as the Law of Moses remained imposed, having standing, there could be no forgiveness, no salvation, no entrance into the Most Holy Place.

The Law of Moses would remain imposed until the time of reformation, when man could have forgiveness and salvation and enter the MHP.

To put this another way, man could have forgiveness and salvation and enter the MHP at the end of Torah, the time of reformation.

But, salvation (and entrance into the MHP) would be at the second appearing of Christ (Hebrews 9:28).

Therefore, the Law of Moses would remain imposed until the time of reformation, the time of the second appearing of Christ —when man could have forgiveness and salvation and enter the MHP.

What all of this means is that if Christ has not come the second time for salvation, there is no entrance into heaven, there is no forgiveness, and the Law of Moses remains valid (Imposed).

Now, it is fascinating to witness the confusion in the evangelical world in regard to entrance into the MHP, i.e. heaven. Even great historical theological figures differed greatly on this issue.

It may not be too much to say that the dominant view in evangelical Christianity today is that when the faithful Christian dies, they go to heaven. Luther and Calvin were both opposed to this:

Martin Luther said:

> As for the popular notion that the souls of the righteous have the full enjoyment of heaven prior to the resurrection, Luther whimsically remarked, 'It would take a foolish soul to desire its body when it was already in heaven!'[36]

He said further: "Now, if one should say that Abraham's soul lives with God but his body is dead, this distinction is rubbish. I will attack it. One must say, 'The whole Abraham, the whole man, shall live.' The other way you tear off a part of Abraham and say, 'It lives.'" (Table Talk, cited by Althaus, op. cit), 447.)

John Calvin likewise opposed the idea that Christians go to heaven prior to the end of time. (John Calvin, *Institutes*, Bk III, chapter 25:6).

---

[36] D. Martin Luthers Werke, ed. Tischreden (Weimar, 1912-1921), 5534, cited by Althaus, op. cit), 417.

On the opposite side stands the Westminster Creed that says: "1. The bodies of men, after death, return to dust, and see corruption; but their souls (which neither die nor sleep), having an immortal subsistence, immediately return to God who gave them. The souls of the righteous, being then made perfect in holiness, are received into the highest heavens, where they behold the face of God in light and glory, waiting for the full redemption of their bodies; and the souls of the wicked are cast into hell, where they remain in torments and utter darkness, reserved to the judgment of the great day. Besides these two places for souls separated from their bodies, the Scripture acknowledgeth none." (*The Westminster Confession* Chapter 32—Of the State of Man After Death, and of the Resurrection of the Dead).

So, we have the two dominant views concerning the fate of the dead. One side says the faithful Christian goes to Hades—Abraham's bosom—to await the resurrection. The other side says the faithful Christian goes to heaven when they die. (There is of course, the view of "soul sleep" as well, but, that is just a modified form of saying that the Christian does not go to heaven until the end of time).

The question is, when could man enter the MHP, heaven, the presence of God? Certain things are clear from Hebrews 9:

1. It could not be while Torah remained valid. Torah had to pass before man could enter the MHP.

2. It could not be until there was forgiveness of sin.

3. It would only be at "the time of reformation."

4. It would only be at the second appearing of Christ, for salvation.

Now, of course, most Christians believe that the saints actually received/receive objective forgiveness prior to the second appearing. But this is not a Biblical doctrine. According to Romans 11:25–27 forgiveness would become a reality at the coming of Christ in judgment. The Holy Spirit was given by the Lord to serve as the guarantee of that coming day of redemption, the coming day of forgiveness. Look carefully at Ephesians 1:7, 4:30:

"In Him we have redemption through His blood, the forgiveness of sins, according to the riches of His grace."

Notice that redemption is explained *as forgiveness*. In fact, many translations render this as, "In whom we have redemption, *even* the forgiveness of sins..." Thus, redemption is forgiveness which is redemption. Of course, if we read the text in isolation from the rest of the book, we might conclude that forgiveness was an actual, objective reality at that time. But, that would be wrong. Notice what Paul goes ahead to say:

"And do not grieve the Holy Spirit of God, by whom you were sealed for the day of redemption."

Now, in chapter 1:12–14, Paul said the Spirit had been given as the *arrabon*, the guarantee of the redemption of the purchased possession. Here in 4:30, he says the Spirit had sealed them for "the day of redemption." So, redemption had not yet come, even though they had received the Spirit as the guarantee that it would come. (See Philippians 1:6 on this). Redemption was an "already–but–not–yet" reality. Let me express it like this:

Redemption is forgiveness (Ephesians 1:7).

The day of redemption was still future when Paul wrote (Ephesians 4:30).

Therefore, forgiveness was yet future when Paul wrote.

This comports perfectly with the imagery of Hebrews 9 that presents Jesus as the Great High Priest making the Atonement. Christ had appeared to offer himself as the sacrifice. He entered the MHP with his blood to offer it there. He would appear the second time to bring salvation—the Atonement perfected! And we must take note that the author said that the second appearing was to be in a "very, very little while, and will not delay" (10:37).

Now, what does the writer posit at the time of salvation, the time of reformation? Entrance into the Most Holy Place because forgiveness is a reality at that second appearing!

The correlation between the second appearing of Christ, entrance into the MHP, the time of reformation, and forgiveness should not be missed. And yet, what happens so often is that commentators say that we have forgiveness, but, we are waiting for salvation! But, if we have forgiveness, we have access to the Presence of God, which is nothing other than salvation! If not, what is the difference between forgiveness, salvation and access to the Presence of the Lord?

Carefully note the following:

∗ While Torah remained imposed there was no forgiveness, and thus, no entrance into the MHP. That meant no *salvation*.

∗ Torah would remain imposed "until the time of reformation."

99

* The time of reformation is the putting right, making correct, the fault and weakness of Torah—where there was no forgiveness, no entrance into the MHP, no salvation.

* Salvation, entrance into the MHP, would come at the second appearing of Christ.

* Therefore, the time of reformation, the time of forgiveness and entrance into the MHP would be at the second appearing of Christ.

Needless to say, if Christ has not come the second time, Torah remains imposed. There is no forgiveness. There is no entrance into the MHP. There is no salvation.

Needless to say, if Christ has not come the second time, Torah remains imposed. There is no forgiveness. There is no entrance into the MHP. There is no salvation. There is no resurrection life!

Take careful note of 2 Corinthians 3, where Paul spoke of the Old Covenant as the "ministration of death, written and engraven in stone" (v. 7). This was the Ten Commandments that Paul was calling the ministration of death. In the ensuing verses, he spoke of then present passing of that ministration of death—"that which is passing away." He said the end of that Old Covenant world remained their "hope" and that hope (since it was still his hope it was not an accomplished reality!) that gave them boldness to speak of its passing, and the greater glory of the New Covenant.

In verse 18 he said that they were at that time, "being transformed, from Glory to Glory." That "Glory transformation" was the transition from the ministration of death to the ministration of life. This is nothing less than resurrection and since Paul said the transformation (literally, *metamorphosis*) was taking place, this means that the resurrection was taking place. The transition from death to life is resurrection, is it not?

Now, how does all of this relate to the Gospel, the good news, of the kingdom and the fall of Jerusalem?

Remember that Jesus and his disciples posited the coming fall of Jerusalem as the "end of the age" (συντελείας τοῦ αἰῶνος, *suntelieas tou aionos* – Matthew 24:3). That temple represented—it was the ultimate of the symbol of—the Covenant. While the destruction of the temple itself did not automatically signify the end of the Covenant (since the Temple was destroyed in BC 586, yet the covenant did not pass at that time), in Matthew, that destruction was to be the sign of the end of the Covenant age of Moses and the Law. And notice that it would be the consummation (singular consummation, *suntelieas* – συντελείας, of "*the* age", *tou aionos* – τοῦ αἰῶνος – singular – Strong's #3588). The disciples knew, based on OT prophecies, that the end of the age was to occur with the judgment on Jerusalem and the Temple.

The Old Covenant age was the age of the "ministration of death, written and engraven in stone." It was the end of the age in which there was no entrance into the Most Holy Place. It was the end of the age in which there was no true forgiveness, and thus, no objective "life" or "righteousness" (Galatians 3:20–21).

In light of all of this, is it difficult to see how Jesus' words about the impending fall of Jerusalem being "the gospel of the kingdom" were in fact true? Was it not—is it not—absolutely true that the passing of the ministration of death would be *fantastic* news? Would not reception of redemption, "even the forgiveness of sin" not be wonderful news (Ephesians 1:7–> 4:30)? Would not the end of the ineffective sacrificial system, giving way to the perfect sacrifice of

101

Jesus, not be thrilling good news? Would not being delivered from the law of sin and death (Romans 8:1–3) be the best news possible?

When one considers everything that scripture has to say about the ineffectiveness, the weakness and the inability of Torah to bring man to God, to provide life, righteousness, forgiveness, a clean conscious, and access to His Presence, how could the news that the destruction of Jerusalem and the Temple, even though that would admittedly be traumatic, not be considered "This gospel (this good news!) of the kingdom"?

How Could Jesus Call the Message of the Impending Fall of Jerusalem, the Gospel (the "Good News!") of the Kingdom?

Point # 9

It was the Consummation of the Eschatological Wrath of God It Was the Time of Redemption!

I want to reiterate here something we noted at the very beginning and that is that when Jesus foretold the preaching of the Gospel into all the world prior to the fall of Jerusalem, he was not simply predicting the preaching of the gospel (generically considered) into all the world in Matthew 24:14. Unfortunately, that is how this text is normally considered. But that is not what he said. He literally said that "this *the* gospel of the kingdom must be preached into all the world." (The Greek is τοῦτος *(this)* τό *(the)* εὐαγγέλιον, euangelion, (ospel or good news)). He was speaking of a very specific bit of "good news."

What was "*this* the gospel" he was referring to? The antecedent discussion shows that it was the message of the impending end of the Old Covenant Age, and the fall of Jerusalem. Jesus was not referring to the Gospel comprehensively considered or defined. It was a very specifically defined bit of "good news" that he was referring to.

That is not to say that the Gospel comprehensively defined was not *included*, because the proclamation of the Gospel of Christ, crucified, buried and resurrected, meant that the New Creation had broken in and was now imminent. That signaled the "beginning of the end" of the Old. Thus, my comments should not, in any sense be construed as saying that the Gospel comprehensively defined was not to be—and was not—preached into the world. My main focus is the immediate context of Matthew 24 that shows that the "good news," *the very specific good news* that Jesus had in mind in Matthew 24:14 was the

103

declaration and prediction of the end of the Old Covenant age. This is important for understanding Jesus' comments in Matthew 24:14. With this in mind, we proceed with our comments.

In our previous discussion I suggested to you that the fall of Jerusalem, the destruction of the Temple, signified the end of the Old Covenant age, the Old Covenant ministration of Death. I shared with you how the NT writers and specifically Hebrews 9, speak of the time still future to them, but coming soon, when all hindrance to man's entrance into the MHP would be realized and fully accessible.

Per the Hebrews writer, the end of the Law of Moses and access and entrance into the MHP, heaven, are inextricably bound together. To explore that, we go to the book of Revelation.

Revelation 11:19

> Then the temple of God was opened in heaven, and the ark of His covenant was seen in His temple. And there were lightnings, noises, thunderings, an earthquake, and great hail.

Notice that the Temple (the naos, ὁ ναὸς – The MHP) of God was seen to be opened. For John to be able to see into the MHP meant the Veil was gone! The implications of this are absolutely profound! One might be tempted, as some are, to jump to the conclusion that since the veil was gone, that man had full access to the MHP before the parousia, before the resurrection. But, that would be to cut short the narrative in Revelation. For brevity, let's move to another text.

Revelation 15:8:

> The temple was filled with smoke from the glory of
> God and from His power, and no one was able to
> enter the temple till the seven plagues of the seven
> angels were completed.

So, here is more of the story of the MHP. John, once again is
privileged to gaze into the MHP. But, notice that there is an "until" to
the story. That "until" tells us that although the Veil was removed,
actual entrance into that Sacred Place was not yet accessible, and it
would not be truly accessible "until the seven plagues of the seven
angels were completed." God's wrath had to be finished before man
could enter the MHP. So, the filling up of God's wrath and entrance
into the Most Holy are temporally linked.

Notice now, briefly, the perfect correlation between the consummation
of the Wrath of God, redemption, and Luke 21:22–28

> For these are the days of vengeance, that all things
> which are written may be fulfilled. But woe to those
> who are pregnant and to those who are nursing babies
> in those days! For there will be great distress in the
> land and wrath upon this people. And they will fall
> by the edge of the sword, and be led away captive
> into all nations. And Jerusalem will be trampled by
> Gentiles until the times of the Gentiles are fulfilled.
> And there will be signs in the sun, in the moon, and
> in the stars; and on the earth distress of nations, with
> perplexity, the sea and the waves roaring; men's
> hearts failing them from fear and the expectation of
> those things which are coming on the earth, for the
> powers of the heavens will be shaken. Then they will

see the Son of Man coming in a cloud with power and great glory. Now when these things begin to happen, look up and lift up your heads, because your redemption draws near.

What is significant is that even Dispensationalists agree that Luke 21:20–24 is about the fall of Jerusalem in AD 70. But, look closer at what that means. It means that the Jewish War was the time for the filling up—the pouring out of God's wrath in fulness. And not only that, it would be at that time, the time of the coming of the Son of Man, when their redemption would be at hand.

Now, it is sometimes argued that the Jesus was using the word "redemption" (Greek – ἀπολύτρωσις, *apolutrosis*, Strong's #629) not in a soteriological sense, but, to refer to their physical deliverance. This word can refer to physical deliverance in some contexts, but that cannot be its meaning here.

Keep in mind that in Matthew 24:15f Jesus had given the disciples signs of his coming in the judgment of Jerusalem. He told them that when they saw the Abomination of Desolation foretold by Daniel the prophet (Daniel 9:26–27/12:9f) they were to flee. In other words, their physical deliverance, their physical redemption, from the horrors of the coming War would take place prior to the actual fall, prior to the destruction! Thus, their "redemption" in verse 28 is not a reference to their physical deliverance. It was the redemption mentioned in Ephesians 1:12–13 and 4:30—the redemption of the purchased possession.

Incredibly, as I shared earlier, some Dispensationalists see, or seemingly see, the incredible importance of AD 70 as the time of vengeance, but, they fail to grasp the implications of their own comments. For instance, read what Thomas Ice says about Luke 21:22,

Luke 21:20 must be A.D. 70 because it speaks of the days of vengeance, and this means "Those first century days are called 'days of vengeance' for Jerusalem is under the divine judgment of covenantal sanctions recorded in Leviticus 26 and Deuteronomy 28." Luke records that God's vengeance upon His elect nation is "in order that all things which are written may be fulfilled." Jesus is telling the nation that God will fulfill all the curses of the Mosaic covenant because of Israel's disobedience. He will not relent and merely bring to pass a partial fulfillment of His vengeance. Some of the passages that Jesus said would be fulfilled include the following: Lev. 26:27–33; Deut. 28:49f; 32:19–27; 1 Kings 9:1–9; Jeremiah 6:1–8; 26:1–9;Daniel 9:26; Hosea 8:1–10; 10:15; Micah 3:12; Zechariah 11:6) (Thomas Ice, (*The Great Tribulation Past or Future?*, (Grand Rapids, MI: Kregel Publications, 1999), 98– cited above).

Do you see what Ice says? AD 70 was the *complete*, not the partial, but the total fulfillment of the curses of the Mosaic Covenant! He then lists numerous texts that he posits as fulfilled in AD 70. Among those is Daniel 9:26. (I cannot take the time to examine each of the texts that Ice posits as fulfilled in AD 70, but, suffice it to say that logically, he has totally surrendered his eschatology!)

Now, Ice and other Dispensationalists, as well as representatives of other futurist views, sometimes object to the idea of AD 70 being the time of redemption because, they say, AD 70 was the time of judgment and vengeance, not the time of salvation. This attempted dichotomy between the time of salvation and the time of judgment is extremely unfortunate, and it is un–Biblical. See my book, *Elijah*

107

Has Come: A Solution to Romans 11:25–27 for an extensive discussion of this issue.

Meredith Kline addressed this. In an excellent article, he pointed out how Daniel 9 foretold the time of destruction of Jerusalem but, that Daniel 9 is dependent on Isaiah chapter 10:20f. He demonstrates the power of that connection, showing that for both Isaiah and Daniel, *the time of judgment was in fact to be the time of the salvation of the remnant:*

> Particularly significant for the meaning of *higbir* in Daniel 9:27 is the use of *gibbor* in Isaiah 9 and 10. Isaiah identified the Messiah, the Son of David, as "the mighty God" of the covenant formula by declaring His name to be *'el gibbor* (Isa. 9:5). Then in Isaiah 10 this messianic *'el gibbor* is mentioned again in the very passage from which Daniel 9:27 derives its thought and wording alike (see verses 21–23). Isaiah spoke there of God's mighty messianic fulfillment of covenant blessing and curse: a remnant of Jacob would return unto *'el gibbor*, but in overflooding (*sotep*) judicial righteousness the annihilation (*kalah*) that was determined (*neherasah*) would befall the land. Daniel 9:26b, 27 echoes Isaiah's prophecy: the covenant would be made to prevail (*higbir*), as a blessing for the many who were the faithful remnant, but as a curse in the form of the determined annihilation (*kalah weneherasah*) which would be poured out on the abominations of apostate Israel like a flood (*setep*). The unmistakable dependence of Daniel 9:27 on Isaiah 10:21ff points directly to the *'el gibbor* of Isaiah 10:21 as the inspiration for the *gabar* of Daniel 9:27.This confirms the conclusions that the

subject of *higbir* is not antichrist or any other than the anointed one whose name is *'el gibbor* and that the object of *higbir*, the covenant made to prevail, is the redemptive covenant sealed by the reconciling blood of Christ [i.e. the New Covenant].[37]

Now, when we realize that the time of the overwhelming flood of destruction of AD 70 was also the time for the bringing in of everlasting righteousness (Daniel 9:24) i.e. the New Creation, are absolutely tied together, we are better equipped to understand how the message of the coming destruction of Jerusalem and the Temple in AD 70 could have been—and was—called "this gospel (this good news) of the kingdom." And to return to Revelation, we can see there that exact conflation of concepts.

Notice again that in Revelation 11 and 15–16, the wrath of God had to be poured out, in full, on the Great Harlot City Babylon, for entrance into the MHP to be open for all men. This conflates redemption (Luke 21:28) with the judgment of that Harlot City that had slain the prophets and was where the Lord was crucified. In fact, Revelation 19 emphatically posits that time of Babylon's destruction as the time of *salvation*:

> After these things I heard a loud voice of a great multitude in heaven, saying, "Alleluia! Salvation and

---

[37] Meredith G Kline, "The Covenant of the Seventieth Week," in *The Law and the Prophets: Old Testament Studies in Honor of Oswald T. Allis* (Nutley, NJ: Presbyterian and Reformed, 1974), 8–9.

glory and honor and power belong to the Lord our God! For true and righteous are His judgments, because He has judged the great harlot who corrupted the earth with her fornication; and He has avenged on her the blood of His servants shed by her." Again they said, "Alleluia! Her smoke rises up forever and ever!" (Revelation 19:1–3).

And of course, this agrees perfectly with what Revelation 11:15f anticipated with the destruction of that city where the Lord was crucified:

Then the seventh angel sounded: And there were loud voices in heaven, saying, "The kingdoms of this world have become the kingdoms of our Lord and of His Christ, and He shall reign forever and ever!" And the twenty–four elders who sat before God on their thrones fell on their faces and worshiped God, saying: "We give You thanks, O Lord God Almighty, The One who is and who was and who is to come, Because You have taken Your great power and reigned."

So, we have in Isaiah, in Daniel, Luke, and in Revelation (in fact, throughout Scriptures), the conflation of salvation and judgment. As we have seen, the time of Israel's destruction would be when the New Creation would arrive. Is the New Creation wonderful news? Who would doubt that? But, was it "bad news" that the Old Covenant form of Israel had to be destroyed in order to bring in that New Creation? Of course! After all, Jesus said that time would be the greatest tribulation of all time. But, the fact that the destruction of Jerusalem was an awful, horrendous time, does not mean that we can divorce that

110

time and those events from the birth of the New Creation, the everlasting kingdom of Christ.

Thus, when Jesus foretold the impending dissolution of the Old Covenant age, with the attendant destruction of Jerusalem, there is no doubt that it was considered "bad news." But, it was also wonderful, awesome news! It means—and means—that the never-ending kingdom of God is now with man. It means that all men are now invited to participate in the salvation that flowed from Israel to the nations. The Old Covenant kingdom was transformed. The earthly house of this tabernacle was "dissolved" (from 2 Corinthians 5:1-3, Greek word: καταλυθῇ, *kataluthe*, Strong's #2647). And now, "The tabernacle of God is with man!" How is this not "the gospel—the good news!—of the Kingdom"?

What we have seen then is that according to the consistent testimony of Scripture, throughout the Tanakh and the NT, the end of the Old Covenant age was to be a traumatic event. It was in fact to be horrific, because it entailed bringing on Israel a holocaust of destruction:

> Just as they have chosen their own ways, And their soul delights in their abominations, So will I choose their delusions, And bring their fears on them; Because, when I called, no one answered, When I spoke they did not hear; But they did evil before My eyes, And chose that in which I do not delight. Hear the word of the Lord, You who tremble at His word: "Your brethren who hated you, Who cast you out for My name's sake, said, 'Let the Lord be glorified, That we may see your joy.' But they shall be ashamed" (Isaiah 66:3–5).

The Lord would slay the Old Covenant rebels, but save a remnant (Isaiah 65:8–13–> Romans 9–11). The Old Covenant form of the

111

nation and people would no longer be "remembered" i.e. covenantally binding. The Lord would create a New People, with a New Name, in the New Creation (Isaiah 65:15–19). It is in this New Creation that God's people now dwell in His presence, and enjoy eternal life.

So, in light of all of the evidence we have adduced for properly understanding Jesus' words in Matthew 24:14, I hope the reader can better understand how and why he could and did call the message of the impending destruction of the City and Temple, "This Gospel of the kingdom."

How Could Jesus Call the Message of the Impending Fall of Jerusalem, the Gospel (the "Good News!") of the Kingdom?

Point # 10

The Fall of Jerusalem—the Capital of the Old Kingdom, Meant the Full Arrival of the New Covenant Kingdom!

J esus' words in Matthew 24:14 are more than a little astounding. Jesus was talking about the dissolution of the Temple, the epi– center of Israel's kingdom, and he said that the prediction of that coming holocaust was "this gospel of the kingdom." In this work, we have been asking how in the world Jesus could refer to that impending disaster as the good news, and now, the question before us is, how was it the good news of the *kingdom*? Wouldn't the destruction of that Temple be the signal sign that the Old Covenant Kingdom was in—to say the least—extreme danger? While I have, to some degree, refrained from citing numerous scholarly sources in documentation of our discussion, I think it good now to share some important concepts that are too often not recognized by modern readers of Scripture.

One of those things that I hope the reader can grasp is the extreme covenantal importance of the Jerusalem Temple. Unfortunately, we Westerners, we Greek–thinking folks, were not raised with an understanding or appreciation of the covenant in the world view of Israel. And nothing expressed that covenantal relationship more powerfully, more eloquently, more beautifully, than the Jerusalem Temple. Notice just a citation or two.

> In systematic treatments of Jewish theology in the past, the notion of covenant was considered to be one among many other more or less equivalent concerns. Lately, not least due to the publication of E.P.

113

Sanders treatment of Judaism, appreciation for the primacy of covenant in Jewish thought has increased considerably, although it is difficult to understand why it should not always have been obvious that covenant was much more than a peripheral matter in the Jewish world. In any event, it is more widely recognized now that it is the other ideas in the theology of a Jewish group that are likely to have been peripheral. If the distinctive ideas of a Jewish writer did not affect his view of covenant, in other words, chances are that these ideas did not play a major role in his total view of things. Of course, even this very valid observation about the importance of covenant can and has been the subject of excesses, but the opposite mistake of tragically overlooking the important place of covenant theology, especially in the writings presently under consideration has been much more common, and could with justification be called one of the more tragic blunders in the history of biblical and Jewish theology.

The problem seems to be that scholars have repeatedly failed to recognize important covenantal thought, largely because many of the characteristic terms of the covenant—like 'life and death' and the language of blessings and curse—have in time (through overuse in theological jargon as well as through loss of original context) undergone a considerable alteration in meaning. As one outstanding example has been the tendency to overlook the covenantal significance of the word 'life,' which has become distanced from its important covenant context, where it originally served to

114

summarize the blessings promised in the covenant
(cf. Deut. 30:15). While the covenantal associations
of this work may be rather subdued in some texts, it
is nevertheless erroneous to simply understand 'life'
in the Greek philosophical sense of *zoe* as either a
natural or divine force (as we have become
sub–conciously accustomed to do). The word (even
in eschatological expressions like 'eternal life')
frequently retains its more Hebraic sense, evoking
both the quantitative and qualitative measure of the
human experience—that is, a good or bad
experience of life.[38]

Now, Elliott is not discussing the fall of Jerusalem and its
significance, but, what he does say can be applied directly to that
event. Covenant was central to the mind–set of Israel. To fail to
comprehend and appreciate the importance of the covenant and how
Jesus' prediction related to that is to fail to "catch the power" of what
Jesus was predicting. It is to miss the relationship of so many NT texts
that speak of that impending end as if it were "the end of the world."
For the Jews, it was the end of the world. *It was the end of their
world*! As Kenneth Gentry says:

> In essence the temple itself is a symbol: it
> symbolizes the *covenantal relationship* of God with
> His people. The heart of the covenant appears in the
> most important promise: 'I will be your God, you will
> be my people. The temple is the special place where

---

[38] Mark Adam Elliott, *The Survivors of Israel: A
Reconsideration of the Theology of Pre–Christian
Judaism*, (Grand Rapids; Eerdmans, 2000), 245f.

God dwells among His people. (2009, 362, his emphasis).

What Gentry is saying here is what I am expressing: the impact on the Jewish mind of the end of the Temple cultus can hardly be over–emphasized. It was *devastating*—and remains so to this very day. Gentry adds:

> The significance of the collapse of Jerusalem and the destruction of the temple in AD 70 is little appreciated by modern Christians. But, AD 70 effectively closes out the old, typological era and removes a major hindrance to the spread of the Christian faith (1999, 64).

Gregory Stevenson offers this to help us understand:

> Destruction of Jerusalem and the temple were redefining moments in Israel's history. It required a reevaluation of the temple and of Israel's self–perception of its identity relative to God and to its place in the world. Without the temple as the locus of God's gracious presence and without the altars to effect atonement and appease God's wrath, how could Israel anymore lay claim to being the Chosen? The temple had so become an enduring symbol of Israel's covenant status as the elect of God that to lose the symbol called the covenant itself into question.[39]

---

[39] Gregory Stevenson, *Power and Place*, (New York; Walter De Gruyter, 2001), 302). Stevenson's book is very

He shares this quote from a rabbi:

> Reacting to the destruction of Jerusalem in 70 C. E.,
> Rabbi Simeon states: "Since the day that the
> Temple was destroyed there has been no day
> without its curse; and the dew has not fallen in
> blessing and the fruits have lost their savour." (Sot.
> 9:12). (2001, 128).

While this kind of quote could be multiplied many times over, I hope this is sufficient to help you understand how utterly devastating Jesus' prediction was, and, how, if possible, the reality of the destruction was to the Jewish world view. We simply fail to understand culture, society and their religion if we fail—or refuse—to understand their love of the Temple, and the covenant it represented and symbolized.

It was the symbol of Torah. It was the expression of their covenant with YHVH. It was the sign of their *election* as God's people. It was the very definition of their *kingdom*! But, as scholars and commentators have noted, the Jews had come to reverence that physical edifice far beyond what the Lord intended. They seemed to value the *buildings* more than their covenant relationships. Even in Jeremiah's day, there was the tendency to believe that as long as the Temple stood, they were free from their covenantal responsibilities of honesty, integrity, compassion and moral decency (Jeremiah 7:5–11). In Jesus' generation, their sin had reached its zenith (Matthew 12:43– 45).

---

helpful for helping the reader get inside the head of ancients in
regard to incredible importance they placed on Temples.

But, they should have heeded their own prophets who foretold that the time was coming when that Old Covenant kingdom would pass away (Hosea 1/Amos 9) and give way to the New Covenant Kingdom of Messiah. As we have shared above, there was a "good news/bad news" aspect of eschatology.

The good (wonderful!) news was that the New Covenant would provide everything that the Old Covenant could never give, life and righteousness (Galatians 3:20–21).

The bad news was that the Old Covenant people had to be destroyed in order to create a New People with a New Name (Psalms 102/Isaiah 65:13f). The Old Covenant had to pass to bring in the New, better covenant (Jeremiah 31). Even some of the leading patristic writers, e.g. Eusebius, recognized this. The Old Temple—no matter how glorious—had to be destroyed in order to fully manifest and establish the New (Isaiah 66).

In other words, what we are saying is that the fall of Jerusalem had everything to do with the "kingdom." It was the passing of the Old Covenant form of the "kingdom" and the full bloom of the New Covenant "kingdom."

In fact, as Jesus expressed it, the events of the fall of Jerusalem were to be the visible "*sign* of the Son of Man in the heavens." What the original Greek of the text signifies is that the visible realities of the end of Jerusalem and the Temple was *the visible sign* that Jesus was now present as King of kings and Lord of lords over his kingdom! Just as under the Tanakh, when YHVH had "come" in judgment of nations, by utilizing other nations to judge them, He was manifested as God, as the King of the Nations. For those who understood and believed, they saw and understood that it was YHVH at work. But, to the unbelievers, they saw the same events but did not understand...until it

118

was too late (Isaiah 26:9f). In those comings of the Lord, those "Days of the Lord" kingdoms came and kingdoms perished. And that is precisely what happened in the judgment of Jerusalem in AD 70. Jesus told his disciples that they would see him coming in power and great glory, in the kingdom, before all of them died (Matthew 16:27–28). And they were to realize that in the fall of Jerusalem "the kingdom of God is near" (Luke 21:28–32). Christ's kingdom was arriving in full bloom—the good news of the Kingdom—the Old Covenant kingdom was passing away in that horrific event.

When we are unaware of the Old Covenant concept of the Day of the Lord as it related to the rise and fall of kingdoms, we will miss the application to Jesus' coming. Jesus said he was going to come in the glory of the Father (in other words, in the same manner as the Father had come), and he was coming in the kingdom. He was coming as the King of kings to judge the Old Covenant kingdom that had rejected him and put him to death. His kingdom was going to supplant and destroy that bloody kingdom. And now, his kingdom is a kingdom that shall never pass away. It will never end. It will never cease to function.

And so, once again, the "Gospel of Destruction" is revealed. Just as Isaiah 65–66 taught, the Old Covenant kingdom would pass away— "the Lord God shall slay you" (65:13). The New Covenant kingdom, the New Creation of Jesus the Messiah, will continue forever, age without end. As believers, we must proclaim the glory of this everlasting kingdom that fully arrived at the end of the Old Covenant ministry of Death, and brought life and immortality to light through the Gospel.

How Could Jesus Call the Message of the Impending Fall of Jerusalem, the Gospel (the "Good News!") of the Kingdom?

Point # 11

Because the End of the Old Covenant Age Was the Time of the Resurrection and New Creation

At the risk of redundancy, I want to explore now the fact that Matthew 24—the very "section" that both Amillennialists and Postmillennialists alike admit referred to the Lord's coming in AD 70—actually contains a powerful prediction of the resurrection of the dead. If this is true—and it is—then when it is admitted that Matthew 24:4–34 is about AD 70, this is a tacit admission that the resurrection is fulfilled.

In the Amillennial and Postmillennial world, the majority view is that Matthew 24–25 discusses two topics, Jesus' spiritual coming in the fall of Jerusalem in AD 70 is discussed in Matthew 24:4–34, and then, in Matthew 24:36–25:46 Jesus supposedly speaks of the "end of the world," "end of time" coming of Christ. We are told that in chapter 25:31f Jesus focused on the final judgment at the time of the resurrection of the dead. (See my recent 15 part YouTube video series in which I respond to Kenneth Gentry's book, Have We Missed the Second Coming? In that book, Gentry presents several "reasons" for his belief that the Olivet Discourse discusses these two different and disparate events).

If you were to ask any of the leading representatives from the Amillennial fellowship in which I was raised, if Matthew 24:4–34 discusses the resurrection of the dead, you would undoubtedly get a somewhat puzzled look followed by a vehement and definitive: "No!" as an answer. The reality, however, is that Matthew 24:4–34 does discuss the resurrection, and does so very powerfully. I will establish that in two ways:

1. By showing that Jesus' discussion of *the Great Tribulation* was tacitly, but, undeniably related to the resurrection.

2. By showing that Jesus' discussion of the gathering of the elect from the four winds *at the sounding of the Great Trumpet* would have been understood—should be understood—as a prediction of the resurrection.

The Resurrection and the Great Tribulation

Let me begin by sharing just a few quotes from leading scholars who recognize that the Great Tribulation was in the first century, inextricably bound up with the Jewish War.

While there are some Amillennialists that believe that the Great Tribulation still lies the future, (e.g Kim Riddlebarger), the majority view is that the Great Tribulation occurred in the first century, in the Jewish War of AD 66–70.

Reformed Amillennialist James Jordan, with whom I had a formal public debate, says: "It is perverse for commentators to continue to insist that the Great Tribulation is still in the future."[40]

---

[40] James Jordan, *The Hand Writing on the Wall*, (Powder Springs, GA; American Vision, 2007), 619.

Postmillennialist Keith Mathison says: "There is no end–time tribulation. Jesus' prophecy about tribulation in Matthew 24 was fulfilled between AD 30 and AD 70."[41]

Likewise, Kenneth Gentry says: "Copious, clear and compelling evidence demonstrates that the great tribulation occurs in the first century."[42]

We could provide extensive additional quotes from both Amillennialists and Postmillennialists who claim that the Great Tribulation was in the first century, immediately prior to and directly related to the end of Israel's Old Covenant Age, but, these quotations are sufficient.

Now, take a look at a very small bit of documentation that shows that scholars likewise recognize the link between the Tribulation and the Resurrection. I am copying some of this from a series of articles that I recently did on Isaiah 66.

Emile Schurer says that in ancient Jewish belief:

> Reference to the last things is almost always accompanied by the notion, recurring in various forms, that a period of special distress and affliction must precede the dawn of salvation...In Rabbinic

---

[41] Keith Mathison, *Dispensationalism: Rightly Dividing the House of God?*, (Phillipsburg, NJ; P & R Publishing, 1995), 144.

[42] Kenneth Gentry, *He Shall Have Dominion*, Draper, VA; Apologetics Group, 2009), 356.

teaching, the doctrine therefore developed of the birth pangs of Messiah which must precede His appearance (the expression is from Hosea 13:13; cf. Matthew 24:8).[43]

Brant Pitre also calls our attention to the fact that in the Hebrew scriptures:

> According to the OT, the resurrection itself would be preceded by "a period of great tribulation"... Daniel 12, which is the most explicit prophecy of resurrection in the Hebrew books of the Old Testament. Strikingly, this description of the resurrection is preceded by the Great Tribulation.[44]

Pitre then offers a summation of the Jewish eschatological narrative that he gleaned from many sources leading up to AD 30. What is so amazing—and significant—is that these tenets and principles listed below are used by Jesus and the apostles and expanded in NT. Jesus' narrative followed the Jewish time line! Here is that time line and narrative that the Jews and Jesus shared:

---

[43] Emile Schurer, *History of the Jewish People in the Age of Jesus Christ*, Vol. II, (London; T and T Clark, 1979), 514.

[44] Brant Pitre, *Jesus, Tribulation and the End of Exile* (Grand Rapids; Baker Academic, 2005), 187.

1. Tribulation is tied to the restoration of Israel which requires an end to exile.

2. The righteous remnant would arise during the tribulation.

3. There will be a righteous Sufferer (individual); and the righteous collectively suffer and/or die during the Tribulation period.

4. The Tribulation is tied to the coming of the Messiah, sometimes referred to as the Son of Man.

5. There is a Tribulation that precedes the Final Judgment.

6. The Tribulation is depicted as the eschatological climax of Israel's exilic sufferings. (from Deuteronomy 28–30 the Law of Blessing and Curses).

7. The Tribulation has two stages: a preliminary stage and then a later greater tribulation.

8. The Tribulation precedes the coming of the eschatological kingdom.

9. An eschatological tyrant opponent or some anti–Messiah arises during the tribulation.

10. Typological images from the Old Testament are used to depict the tribulation (symbology, imagery).

11. The tribulation is tied to the ingathering and/or the conversion of the Gentiles.

12. The tribulation has some kind of an atoning or a redemptive function.

13. The Jerusalem temple is defiled and/or destroyed during the Tribulation.

14. The tribulation precedes the resurrection of the dead and a new creation.

At one time, Sam Frost taught this truth, and saw that Daniel 12:1–2 tied the Tribulation to the time of the resurrection. In his excellent *Exegetical Essays on the Resurrection*, Frost even argued from the linguistic and grammatical evidence of Daniel 12:1–2 that the Tribulation and the Resurrection cannot be divorced temporally: "It is clear that both the Hebrew *waw* and the Greek *kai* (and) connect vv. 1 and 2."[45] Frost now rejects his own grammatical argument and claims that the Hebrew *waw* and the Greek *kai*, are "simple connectives." Well, yes, *that is true!* That is the point! But that means that those "simple connectives" connect verse 1 with verse 2, thereby falsifying Frost's current claims.

---

[45] Sam Frost, *Exegetical Essays on the Resurrection*, (Ardmore, Ok; JaDon Management Inc. 2010), 119. In several FaceBook exchanges with Frost since his departure from the full preterist view, Frost has changed his views on Daniel 12:2 several times. His latest (2017) is that Daniel 12:1 was fulfilled in the time of Antiochus Epiphanes, but that verse 2 is the end of human history resurrection. When I have challenged him to give any kind of linguistic, grammatical, contextual justification for that claim, he has refused to offer it, other than to simply affirm that verse 2 must refer to a literal, physical resurrection of bodies out of the literal dust.

The indisputable reality is that scripturally, the Great Tribulation and the Resurrection are indeed temporally connected. That being true, it means that since the Olivet Discourse predicted the Great Tribulation and the coming of the Lord, it likewise foretold the resurrection. This is utterly devastating to the Amillennial and Postmillennial schools that openly admit, as just seen, that the Great Tribulation was in the first century.

Now, please catch the power of the following:

The Great Tribulation would lead directly to, would usher in the Resurrection.

But, the Great Tribulation was to be in the first century, in direct connection to the Jewish War of AD 66–70—It would be in Jesus' generation (Matthew 24:34)

Therefore, the Great Tribulation would occur in Jesus' generation.

****

Let's follow that with this:

The Great Tribulation would occur in Jesus' generation.

But, the Great Tribulation would usher in the Resurrection.

Therefore, the Great Tribulation of Jesus' generation would usher in the Resurrection—it would be in Jesus' generation.

In my public debate with Dr. David Hester, of Faulkner University, in June 2017, in Montgomery, Alabama, I raised the issue of the

Tribulation and the Resurrection. I demonstrated that Daniel 12:1–2 tie those two events together and that in verse 7 we are told that "all of these things" would be fulfilled "when the power of the holy people is completely shattered" (v. 7). I shared that Dr. Hester believes that the Great Tribulation occurred in the first century, and was during the Jewish War of AD 66–70. That demands that the resurrection was in the first century.

Dr. Hester was clearly shaken with the argument. He had initially said that Daniel 12:2 is the end of time resurrection. But, confronted with verse 7 he then changed his position and said that Daniel 12:2 is not the same resurrection of 1 Corinthians 15. He even went so far as to say that the resurrection of Daniel 12 is not the same as John 5:28–29! When I demonstrated the direct parallels between Daniel 12 and 1 Corinthians 15, he changed position *again* and said that Daniel might be the end–time resurrection, but, it was not fulfilled in AD 70! When I pointed out that his position demands the destruction of the Gospel—God's power to save—he never said another word about Daniel 12. His vacillation was manifested to everyone.[46]

---

[46] A book of our first debate [of two debates] entitled *The Resurrection of the Just and Unjust*, is available from my websites, Amazon, Kindle and other retailers. There was no doubt in anyone's mind that Dr. Hester realized that the connection of the Tribulation to the Resurrection was fatal to his eschatology.

See my book, *The Resurrection of Daniel 12:2: Future or Fulfilled?*[47] for extensive documentation of the relationship—the inter–connectedness—between the Tribulation and the Resurrection. In short, in the OT scriptures, in text after text, we find the Tribulation foretold and following hard on that prediction is the subsequent Resurrection. Here are just a few examples:

Jeremiah 30:1–10:

> The word that came to Jeremiah from the Lord, saying, "Thus speaks the Lord God of Israel, saying: 'Write in a book for yourself all the words that I have spoken to you. For behold, the days are coming,' says the Lord, 'that I will bring back from captivity My people Israel and Judah,' says the Lord. 'And I will cause them to return to the land that I gave to their fathers, and they shall possess it.'" Now these are the words that the Lord spoke concerning Israel and Judah. For thus says the Lord: "We have heard a voice of trembling, Of fear, and not of peace. Ask now, and see, Whether a man is ever in labor with child? So why do I see every man with his hands on his loins Like a woman in labor, And all faces turned pale? Alas! For that day is great, So that none is like it; And it is the time of Jacob's trouble, But he shall be saved out of it. 'For it shall come to pass in that day,' Says the Lord of hosts, 'That I will break his

---

[47] Don K. Preston, *The Resurrection of Daniel 12:2: Fulfilled or Future?* (Ardmore, Ok; JaDon Management Inc., 2016). The book is available on Amazon, my websites, Kindle and other retailers.

yoke from your neck, And will burst your bonds; Foreigners shall no more enslave them. But they shall serve the Lord their God, And David their king, Whom I will raise up for them. Therefore do not fear, O My servant Jacob,' says the Lord, 'Nor be dismayed, O Israel; For behold, I will save you from afar, And your seed from the land of their captivity. Jacob shall return, have rest and be quiet, And no one shall make him afraid."

.——Notice that this passage foretold the restoration of the whole house of Israel, Judah and the ten tribes.

.——While it foretold the restoration of Israel, it likewise posited that restoration at the time of birth pains, the time of Jacob's trouble. It would be a time like no other! Sound familiar? It should, because it is repeated by Daniel 12:1 and by Jesus in Matthew 24.

Now, if in fact, Daniel 12:1 is echoing Jeremiah, then the claim by Sam Frost that Daniel 12:1 was fulfilled in the time of Antiochus Epiphanes is falsified. After all, even Frost would not claim that "all Israel" (i.e. all twelve tribes) was restored in the time of Antiochus. Not only that, but in Jeremiah 30, at the time of that Great Tribulation the Messiah would be raised up: "They shall serve the Lord their God, and David their king, whom I will raise up for them" (v. 9). This is patently a Messianic, kingdom prophecy, just as Daniel 12:1–3 foretold the time of the Tribulation, the time of the end and the time of the kingdom. So, unless Frost is willing to say that the Messiah came and established the kingdom in the time of Antiochus, his view is falsified.

These passages and others provided the scriptural source for the Jewish understanding that the Great Tribulation would give way to the

Resurrection. This was the normative timeline in Jewish eschatology. Scholarship has long recognized this connection.

With these thoughts in mind, let's turn now to Jesus' reference to the gathering of the elect at the sounding of "the Great Trumpet." This was a powerful prediction of the resurrection!

The Resurrection At the Sounding of the Great Trumpet

Isaiah 27:7–8:

> Has He struck Israel as He struck those who struck him? Or has He been slain according to the slaughter of those who were slain by Him? In measure, by sending it away, You contended with it. He removes it by His rough wind in the day of the east wind.

In this text, Israel is depicted as slain, dead, *by being sent away into captivity*. Let that soak in: God said He had (*past tense*) killed them "by sending them away" into captivity. They were physically alive, living in the foreign countries to which they were scattered, but in the eyes of the Lord (and themselves), they were dead.

Notice then that the Lord made a promise in verse 13:

> So it shall be in that day: The great trumpet will be blown; They will come, who are about to perish in the land of Assyria, And they who are outcasts in the land of Egypt, And shall worship the Lord in the holy mount at Jerusalem.

This text has almost always been considered a "resurrection text" by the ancient Rabbis and many commentators. And little wonder. The

130

Lord had slain the "dispersed" by sending them away, but, at the sounding of the Great Trumpet, he would regather "those who were about to perish."

Mitch and Zhava Glaser, say, "The holy one, Blessed be He, will sound the shofar at the time of the ingathering of the exiles of Israel to their place" (Isaiah 27:13) (citing Eliyahu Zuta 2). (1987, 22–23).

Greg Beale commenting on 1 Corinthians 15:52 and the sounding of the Trumpet at the time of the resurrection that it is an echo of Isaiah 27:13.[48]

John Nolland, says that Matthew 24:31 is drawing on Zechariah 9:14 and Isaiah 27:13.[49]

Likewise, Donald Hagner says: "The reference to the blowing of the Great Trumpet in connection with the gathering of the righteous is found in Isaiah 27:13 (in the NT reference to the eschatological trumpet occurs in conjunction with the descent from heaven in 1

---

[48] Greg Beale, *Commentary on the NT Use of the OT,* (Grand Rapids; Baker Academic, Apollos, 2007), 747.

[49] John Nolland, *New International Greek Text Commentary, Matthew,* (Grand Rapids; Eerdmans, Paternoster, 2005), 985.

Thessalonians 4:16; there, as in 1 Corinthians 15:52 the trumpet is associated with the resurrection of the dead."[50]

The Lord himself applied Isaiah 27:13 in Matthew 24:29–31, and commentators have noted that connection. It is interesting that Gary DeMar takes note of the relationship between Isaiah 27 and Matthew 24:31. He says:

> "When Israel was in captivity, we are told that 'a great trumpet' was blown and those 'who were perishing in the land of Assyria and who were scattered in the land of Egypt, will come and worship the Lord in the holy mountain at Jerusalem (Isaiah 27:13). The 'gathering' most likely refers to the bringing into 'one new man' (Ephesians 2:15) in Christ a body of believers made up of believing Jews and Gentiles (2:17–22), 'that he might gather (*sunagogee*) together into one the children of God who are scattered abroad' (John 11:47–53)."[51]

DeMar fails to note that Israel in captivity was "dead" (Isaiah 27:9f / Ezekiel 37). Thus, the sounding of the Trumpet to gather the elect is nothing less than resurrection.

---

[50] Donald Hagner, *Word Biblical Commentary, Matthew 14–28, Vol. 33b*, (Dallas, Word Publishers, 1995), 714.

[51] Gary DeMar, *Wars and Rumors of Wars,* (Powder Springs, Ga; American Vision, 2017), 195.

On page 147, DeMar comments on the meaning of the Trumpet, and I would suggest that he refutes his own position on the seventy week countdown. He says that the fate of the city described in Daniel 9 lies outside the seventy week countdown. However, in his Wars book just cited, he says that the sounding of the Trumpet of Matthew 24:31 occurred in AD 70, and that it signified "the announcement of the final Jubilee, and the once–for–all–atonement for sin." If this is true— and I believe that it is—then the atonement was not consummated until AD 70. But, this demands that the seventieth week did not end until then, since Daniel 9:24 is clear that "seventy weeks are determined...to make the Atonement."

While Isaiah 27 is speaking of the ten northern tribes, it is parallel in thought to Ezekiel 37 that we will examine below. The fact is that in Hebraic thought, to be separated from the Land, the City and the Temple was to be *dead*. John Watts takes note of this:

> "The exiles in Assyria and Egypt are said to have been perishing. But they will be gathered by God to come and worship him on his holy mountain in Jerusalem (v. 13). Separation from the temple is equivalent to death. Being allowed to participate again in Jerusalem is like coming back to life."[52]

It is unfortunate that far too many Bible students are not familiar with ancient Hebraic thought in this regard.

Notice how the Lord himself applied Isaiah 27:13 in Matthew 24:29–31:

---

[52] John Watts, *Word Biblical Commentary, Isaiah, Vol 24*, (Waco; Word, 1985), 344.

Immediately after the tribulation of those days the sun will be darkened, and the moon will not give its light; the stars will fall from heaven, and the powers of the heavens will be shaken. Then the sign of the Son of Man will appear in heaven, and then all the tribes of the earth will mourn, and they will see the Son of Man coming on the clouds of heaven with power and great glory. And He will send His angels with a great sound of a trumpet, and they will gather together His elect from the four winds, from one end of heaven to the other.

So, Jesus anticipated the fulfillment of Isaiah 27:13 at his coming with the sounding of the Great Trumpet. But, in Matthew 24:34, Jesus, in words too clear to deny, said that all of those things would be fulfilled in his generation. Let me express my thoughts like this:

Isaiah 27:13 foretold the resurrection at the sound of the Great Trumpet.

Jesus said that Isaiah 27:13 would be fulfilled at his coming, with the sounding of the Great Trumpet, at the judgment of Jerusalem, in the first century generation (Matthew 24:31–34).

Therefore, the resurrection at the sounding of the Great Trumpet was fulfilled at the judgment of Jerusalem, in the first century generation.

We need to take a brief, closer look at the Old Covenant prediction of the resurrection at the sounding of the Great Trumpet since the NT utilizes that motif and theme.

It seems to have escaped the notice of many Bible students that the Old Covenant contains the background prophecy of the sounding of the trumpet of God. As we just noted, in Isaiah 27:12–13 Jehovah promised:

> And it shall come to pass in that day that the Lord will thresh, from the channel of the River to the Brook of Egypt; and you will be gathered one by one, O you children of Israel. So it shall be in that day that the great trumpet will be blown. They will come, who are about to perish in the land of Assyria, and they who are outcasts in the land of Egypt, and shall worship the Lord in the holy mount of Jerusalem.

Please note, Isaiah says the trumpet of God would sound and the outcasts of Israel would be gathered. There are some very important facts to be noted here.

First, Isaiah is simply reiterating his earlier promise of the regathering of the scattered people of God, i.e., the remnant. This is a very prominent concept of the Messianic predictions.

In Isaiah 11 the priestly prophet spoke of the day when the ensign would be raised, Gentiles would be saved, and: "It shall come to pass in that day that the Lord shall set his hand again the second time to recover the remnant of his people who are left from Assyria, and Egypt, from Pathros...He will set up a banner for the nations and will assemble the outcasts of Israel, and gather together the dispersed of Judah from the four corners of the earth" (v.11–12). The dispersed would come for "There will be a highway for the remnant of his people who will be left from Assyria, As it was for Israel in the day that he came up from the land of Egypt" (v.16).

Second, it is vital to understand that in the imagery of the prophets, those who were scattered abroad were *dead*; not physically to be sure, but *dead because of separation from God's presence in the Holy Land*! Israel's sin had *separated* between her and God, Isaiah 59:1–2. When he drove them into the foreign countries they were dead because "life" for Israel existed only in fellowship with God in their land, city, and temple. *Death is separation!*[53]

This is found in a brief study of the wider context of Isaiah 27. In chapter 24 God views creation as destroyed because Israel had "transgressed the laws..., broken the everlasting covenant" (v.5). In spite of the punishment, there is promise of deliverance. A great banquet will be prepared for the faithful and he will destroy the veil of destruction; "he will swallow up death forever, And the Lord God will wipe away tears from all faces; the rebuke of His people he will take away from all the earth" (25:6–8).

Chapter 26 offered peace to the repentant. It is said His enemies are dead and will not arise, yet of God's "dead" it is said, "Your dead shall live; together with my dead body they shall arise. Awake and sing, you who dwell in the dust..." (v.19). These "dead" are those taken into captivity by the invaders. This is confirmed in chapter 27:7 when he asks, "Has he struck Israel as he struck those who struck him? Or has he (Israel, DKP) been slain according to the

---

[53] For a powerful examination of the nature and identity of "the death" that was to be overcome at the coming of Christ and the resurrection, get my book, *The Death of Adam/The Life of Christ* (Ardmore, Ok.; 2019). This groundbreaking work shows that biological death was never the focus of the resurrection promises, but rather, the "death" of alienation and separation from God. The book is available on my websites, Amazon, Kindle and other retailers.

slaughter of those who were slain by him?" Israel, carried into captivity, was seen as dead.

This same motif is depicted in Ezekiel's famous vision of the valley of dry bones in chapter 37. The vision is set in the context of Israel's Babylonian captivity. God interprets the vision: "these bones are the whole house of Israel...They indeed say, 'Our bones are dry, our hope is lost, and we ourselves are cut off.'" But God promised, "Behold, O my people, I will open your graves and cause you to come up from your graves, and bring you to the land of Israel." Once again Israel's return from captivity is depicted as the resurrection from the dead because they are being returned to God's fellowship in His land.

This then is the concept of Isaiah 27:13—the Great Trumpet of God was to sound and gather God's elect, in the "grave" of captivity because of the sin of the nation, back to life and fellowship with Jehovah. In the New Testament, the sounding of the trumpet of God is also for the raising of the dead from captivity to be gathered to life with God.

When one follows the NT development of the Sounding of the Trumpet, it soon becomes apparent that neither the Trumpet, nor the resurrection that it would herald, are references to literal, physical realities.[54]

---

[54] Be sure to get a copy of my book, *The Resurrection of Daniel 12:2: Fulfilled or Future?* noted above. This is an incredible and persuasive examination of the doctrine of the resurrection.

To drive this point home, one needs to see the tight connection between the sounding of the Trumpet and the Resurrection.

1 Corinthians 15:51–52

> Behold, I tell you a mystery: We shall not all sleep, but we shall all be changed—in a moment, in the twinkling of an eye, at the last trumpet. For the trumpet will sound, and the dead will be raised incorruptible, and we shall be changed.

Paul spoke of the resurrection, "in a moment, in the twinkling of an eye, at the last trumpet: for the trumpet will sound, and the dead will be raised incorruptible..." (v.52).

Paul says *the trumpet*. He obviously was alluding to some well–known teaching about "the trumpet." Were he introducing a new concept about the sounding of a trumpet would he not have to delineate between the teaching *already known* and the new teaching he was introducing? What was the previous teaching about the sounding of "the trumpet" for the gathering of the dead? It is Matthew 24 and Isaiah 27:13.

Now if it be admitted that the trumpet of Matthew 24 cannot refer to the end of time and creation, and yet it is insisted I Corinthians 15:52 does refer to such, it must clearly be shown why the trumpet of Corinthians is not the same as that in Matthew when Paul simply refers to "the trumpet" and the only sounding of the trumpet mentioned in the New Testament before Corinthians is Matthew 24. One must explain why Matthew is apocalyptic and spiritual language, yet Corinthians is literal/audible; even though 1 Corinthians is patently drawing upon earlier teaching about "the trumpet."

138

The apostle also said it was "the last trumpet." There would be no more trumpets sounded after the "last trumpet." One is almost forced to think of Revelation and the sounding of the 7 trumpets. More on that momentarily.

Observe that Paul emphatically tells us that the resurrection at the sounding of the last trumpet would be the fulfillment of the prediction found in Isaiah 25:8, the very context of the sounding of the great trumpet of God for the gathering of the elect from their "graves," separated from God. Paul says the resurrection of which he speaks was when the strength of sin, i.e., "the law," would be overcome.

Let us not forget that for Paul, "the law" that was the strength of sin was Torah, the law of Moses (Romans 7:7f). That term is used some 128 times in 100 verses. That is "the law" that he called the ministration of death and a covering over the people (cf. Isa.25:7, 2 Cor. 3). It was the law that condemned and cursed (Gal. 3:10–13). It was the law of bondage (Galatians 4:22f). Thus, just as Jesus foretold the end of the Old Covenant age at the dissolution of the Temple and the destruction of the city, Paul anticipated the end of that Old Covenant age—at the resurrection.

When did Paul say the last trumpet was to sound? In verse 51 he says, "we shall not all sleep, but we shall all be changed." This is nothing less than a positive assertion that "This generation shall not pass till all these things be fulfilled." This is parallel to "some standing here shall not taste of death until they see the Son of Man coming in his kingdom" (Matthew 16:27–28).

So, just like in the Olivet Discourse, in I Corinthians 15 we find Christ's coming, judgment, the sounding of the trumpet, the kingdom and the gathering of the elect, i.e., the resurrection. Jesus said those things would be in his generation; Paul said, "we shall not all sleep."

1 Thessalonians 4:16–17

> For the Lord Himself will descend from heaven with
> a shout, with the voice of an archangel, and with the
> trumpet of God. And the dead in Christ will rise first.
> Then we who are alive and remain shall be caught up
> together with them in the clouds to meet the Lord in
> the air. And thus we shall always be with the Lord.

It is critical to see the direct relationship between 1 Thessalonians 4 and the Olivet Discourse. Commentators have long recognized these direct parallels. When we honor them, it is undeniable that Paul is drawing directly from the Olivet Discourse, and more specifically, he is drawing directly from the "section" that both Amillennialists and Postmillennialists agree speaks only of the coming of the Lord in AD 70.

Notice the parallels[55].

V In Matthew 24:29f we have the coming of the Lord –> In Thessalonians we have the coming of the Lord.

V In Matthew 24:29f we have the coming of the Lord with the angels–> In Thessalonians we have the coming of the Lord with the angels.

---

[55] For a chart listing over 20 parallels between the Discourse and Thessalonians, see my, *We Shall Meet Him In The Air: The Wedding of the King of kings,* (Ardmore, Ok; JaDon Management Inc., 2010). The book is available on my websites, Amazon, Kindle and other retailers.

V In Matthew 24:29f we have the coming of the Lord on the clouds of heaven –> In Thessalonians we have the coming of the Lord on the clouds of heaven.

V In Matthew 24:29f we have the coming of the Lord at the sounding of the Trumpet –> In Thessalonians we have the coming of the Lord with the sounding of the Trumpet.

V In Matthew 24:29f we have the coming of the Lord with the sounding of the Trumpet, to gather the elect–> In Thessalonians we have the coming of the Lord with the sounding of the Trumpet to gather the elect.

I would also note that in Matthew 24:31 Jesus used a very rare Greek word, *episunagogee*, to speak of the gathering of the elect. Likewise, Paul, in 2 Thessalonians 2, used that same rare word to speak of the gathering of the Lord at the parousia of Christ.

It seems to me that any impartial reading and examination of these parallels is powerfully persuasive that in Matthew and in Thessalonians, the subject is the same.

Here is the argument that I ask you to consider:

Paul's eschatology in 1 Thessalonians 4 is taken directly from Jesus' teaching on eschatology in Matthew 24:29–34.

Jesus' teaching on eschatology in Matthew 24:29–34 is concerned with his coming at the end of the Old Covenant age of Israel in AD 70.

Therefore, Paul's teaching on eschatology in Thessalonians is concerned with Christ's coming at the end of the Old Covenant age of Israel in AD 70.

This means, unequivocally, that the resurrection at the sounding of the Trumpet in 1 Thessalonians 4 was at the end of the Old Covenant world of Israel in AD 70.

Revelation 11:15–19

> Then the seventh angel sounded: And there were loud voices in heaven, saying, "The kingdoms of this world have become the kingdoms of our Lord and of His Christ, and He shall reign forever and ever!" And the twenty–four elders who sat before God on their thrones fell on their faces and worshiped God, saying:

> We give You thanks, O Lord God Almighty, The One who is and who was and who is to come, Because You have taken Your great power and reigned. The nations were angry, and Your wrath has come, And the time of the dead, that they should be judged, And that You should reward Your servants the prophets and the saints, And those who fear Your name, small and great, And should destroy those who destroy the earth.

Very clearly, what we have in Revelation 11 is another version of Matthew 24.

We can't lose sight of the fact that the sounding of the seventh angel is the sounding of the seventh—the last—trump (Revelation 10:6f).

Revelation 8–11

John saw seven angels having seven trumpets. Beginning with chapter 8 those angels sounded their trumpets. In chapter 10, John was told, "in the days of the voice of the seventh angel, when he shall begin to sound, the mystery of God should be finished as he hath declared to his servants the prophets." The seventh trumpet, the LAST TRUMPET, was the time for the final fulfilling of the Old Covenant prophetic word.

What was to happen when the last trumpet sounded? In chapter 11:15–19 we are told, "And the nations were angry, and thy wrath is come, and the time of the dead, that they should be judged, and that thou shouldest give reward unto thy servants the prophets, and to the saints..." (v.18). The sounding of the last trumpet was the time for the resurrection of the dead, for judgment.

When was all this to happen? Repeatedly John was told his vision "must shortly come to pass" (1:1–3) and "the time is at hand," (cf. chapter 22:6,10,12,20). In chapter 6 the martyrs who had suffered for their faith were assured they would have to wait only "for a little while" before being vindicated (6:9f).

But, notice that right there in chapter 11 we are given the direct context for this trumpet blast, the judgment and the resurrection. It would be, according to verse 8, at the judgment of the city "where the Lord was crucified." Thus, the context and framework for the sounding of the eschatological Trumpets is firmly and undeniably established.

143

Point # 12

Special Study: Matthew 8:11:
Jesus, Abraham, the Kingdom, and the Resurrection

I want to add a bit of corroborating material here not found in the Kindle version of this book. I want to call the reader's attention to Matthew 8:10–11:

> When Jesus heard it, He marveled, and said to those who followed, "Assuredly, I say to you, I have not found such great faith, not even in Israel! And I say to you that many will come from east and west, and sit down with Abraham, Isaac, and Jacob in the kingdom of heaven."

This is an incredibly important resurrection text, yet in my personal experience, I have found that it is somewhat ignored, or even de–emphasized. Why is it so important?

Jesus talks about Abraham, Isaac, and Jacob sitting at the "table" in the kingdom. This ties the kingdom, the resurrection and the AD 70 judgment directly and inseparably together. And we should note that Isaiah 25, one of Paul's source texts for his resurrection doctrine in 1 Corinthians 15, serves as the prophetic backdrop for Matthew 8 as well:

> O Lord, You are my God. I will exalt You, I will praise Your name, For You have done wonderful things; Your counsels of old are faithfulness and truth. For You have made a city a ruin, A fortified city a ruin, A palace of foreigners to be a city no more; It will never be rebuilt. Therefore the strong

people will glorify You; The city of the terrible nations will fear You. For You have been a strength to the poor, A strength to the needy in his distress, A refuge from the storm, A shade from the heat; For the blast of the terrible ones is as a storm against the wall. You will reduce the noise of aliens, As heat in a dry place; As heat in the shadow of a cloud, The song of the terrible ones will be diminished. And in this mountain The Lord of hosts will make for all people A feast of choice pieces, A feast of wines on the lees, Of fat things full of marrow, Of well–refined wines on the lees. And He will destroy on this mountain The surface of the covering cast over all people, And the veil that is spread over all nations. He will swallow up death forever, And the Lord God will wipe away tears from all faces; The rebuke of His people He will take away from all the earth; For the Lord has spoken. And it will be said in that day: "Behold, this is our God; We have waited for Him, and He will save us. This is the Lord; We have waited for Him; We will be glad and rejoice in His salvation" (Isaiah 25:1–9).[56]

A few points to observe:

☐ The context is the time of the destruction of the city and temple (v. 1–3).

---

[56] Scholarship is virtually united and unanimous in agreement that Isaiah 25 serves as the source of Matthew 8:11.

☐ In v. 6 we find the prophecy of the "Messianic Banquet" which is the Wedding Banquet, and the "Table" of the Kingdom in Matthew 8:11. To put it another way, the Banquet is the Resurrection Banquet, since the Banquet is on Mt. Zion where death is abolished (v. 8.)

☐ Death is swallowed up (v. 8). This is the very verse that Paul cited as a prediction of the resurrection in 1 Corinthians 15:55–56.

☐ The time of the Resurrection Banquet when death would be swallowed up, is the day of salvation, and specifically, the time of Israel's salvation (v. 9).

☐ A critical note here by way of repetition and emphasis: the time of the Banquet and Resurrection is the time of the judgment of Jerusalem and the Temple. It is the time of the judgment of the people who had "violated the everlasting covenant" (Isaiah 24:4–5). It is the judgment of "the people," dwelling in "the city," in the midst of "the land" (24:10f). To suggest that this is anyone other than Old Covenant Israel simply has no textual support.

I will make my point as succinctly as possible:

The time of the Banquet of Isaiah 25 is the time of the resurrection of 1 Corinthians 15.

The time of the resurrection is when Abraham and the faithful would sit at the Banquet (Matthew 8:11).

The time of the Banquet would be at the time of the judgment of the people who had "transgressed the everlasting covenant" i.e. Old Covenant Israel (Isaiah 24:1–5; 25:1–6).

146

Therefore, the time of the resurrection, (of 1 Corinthians 15) when Abraham and the faithful would sit at the Banquet would be at the time of the judgment of the people who had "transgressed the everlasting covenant" i.e. Old Covenant Israel (Isaiah 24:1–5; 25:1–6).

Notice how this agrees perfectly with Matthew 8:11. Jesus said that Abraham and the Worthies would sit down at the Banquet Table— the Resurrection Banquet Table, with those from the east and west (which included Gentiles like the Roman Centurion)—"when the sons of the kingdom are cast out." There can be little doubt about when that was, and that is recognized by many commentators.

Kenneth Gentry offered this on Matthew 8:11f –

> "In fact, the dark clouds of the 'day of the Lord' in AD 70 hang over much of the New Testament. God is preparing to punish His people Israel, remove the temple system, and reorient redemptive history from one people and land to all peoples through the earth" (Matthew 8:10–11; 21:43). (2009, 342).[57]

---

[57] Some Amillennialists differ with the Dominionist view of Matthew 8 and insist that it refers to the "end of time." Kim Riddlebarger, *A Case for Amillennialism*, (Grand Rapids; Baker Academic, 2003), 111, dismisses any connection between the text and the judgment of Israel. He applies the casting out of the "sons of the kingdom" to unbelievers, generically speaking. To ignore the referent to the "sons of the kingdom" and simply refer it to "unbelievers" being cast out, is to ignore the *sitz em leben* in which Jesus spoke and "moralize" the text in an entirely inappropriate way. Audience relevance flies out the window.

So, what we have is the affirmation that Matthew 8:11 was fulfilled in AD 70. Lamentably these commentators fail to see the significance of the fact that the "sons of the kingdom" being cast out, is synchronous with Abraham, Isaac, and Jacob sitting down *at the Messianic Banquet*—the time of the resurrection per Isaiah 25:6–8. (Jesus' parallel words recorded in Luke 13 make this connection even more graphically and powerfully).

Logically and contextually, when commentators agree that Matthew 8:11 was fulfilled in AD 70 they are affirming the fulfillment of *Isaiah 25—and thus, 1 Corinthians 15*. Let me illustrate.

Isaiah foretold the coming Banquet that would be established "in this mountain" i.e. Zion. And of course, "Zion" is seen in Hebrews 11–12 as the consummation of the hope of Abraham (Hebrews 12:21f). The connection between Zion and the resurrection cannot be denied.

As suggested above, Isaiah 25 is one of the foundational texts for Paul's resurrection doctrine, (1 Corinthians 15:54–56). In other words, *the resurrection that Paul anticipated was the resurrection foretold by Isaiah 25*. Let me express the connections that are so important to see:

The resurrection foretold by Isaiah 25 would be at the time of the Messianic Banquet (the time of the resurrection of 1 Corinthians 15).

The Messianic Banquet would be when Abraham, Isaac, and Jacob sat down in the kingdom.

Therefore, the time when Abraham, Isaac, and Jacob would sit down in the kingdom would be at the time of the resurrection of 1 Corinthians 15.

Few would doubt that the time under consideration in Isaiah 25 and 1 Corinthians 15 is the time of *the final resurrection to eternal life*. It is the end of the Intermediate State of the Dead.[58] But this means that *Matthew 8:11f* likewise foretold the "final resurrection." So, let me put it like this:

The Messianic Banquet would be when Abraham, Isaac, and Jacob sat down in the kingdom.

The time when Abraham, Isaac, and Jacob would sit down in the kingdom would be at the resurrection (Isaiah 25:6–8; the resurrection of 1 Corinthians 15)—the end of the Intermediate State of the Dead.[59]

---

[58] Incredibly, Joel McDurmon, in our debate, argued that simply because the word "final" is not found in Isaiah 25, it cannot be argued that Isaiah actually predicted the, well, "final resurrection." Such was his desperation to defend a futurist eschatology *on the absence of one word*! I call this the "Missing Elements Hermeneutic" and nothing could be more misguided.

[59] It is stunning to realize that heaven is viewed by some Amillennialists and Postmillennialists as the Intermediate State of the Dead. After all, they tell us that while the righteous go to heaven when they die, they are in fact waiting to come back to earth, to get their physical bodies and then live on earth in a physical kingdom! In this view, heaven is "okay," but, it is not the true hope of the saints—which of course violates Hebrews 6:19–20.

149

But Abraham, Isaac, and Jacob would sit down in the kingdom at the Messianic Banquet when, "the sons of the kingdom" were cast out in AD 70.

Therefore, Abraham, Isaac, and Jacob sat down in the kingdom at the Messianic Banquet, in the final resurrection, (the resurrection of Isaiah 25:6–8; 1 Corinthians 15) when the sons of the kingdom were cast out in AD 70.

Matthew 8 is patently about the fulfillment of the Abrahamic resurrection promises.[60] We cannot fail to note that Matthew 8 and Hebrews 11 are parallel in their discussion of the Abrahamic resurrection promise. Both are discussing the end of the "Intermediate State" of the dead, since they discuss the resurrection to eternal life.

What simply cannot be missed or dismissed is that the fulfillment of Abraham's resurrection promise/hope in Matthew 8 is nothing less than the fulfillment of Isaiah 25—and thus, of 1 Corinthians 15. *And that means that Matthew 8 is depicting the fulfillment of Psalms 110.*[61] (I am only mentioning Psalms 110 briefly here, but, see my book on Luke 19 and its relationship to the Psalm).

---

[60] The connection between the Messianic Banquet, the resurrection and Matthew 8:11 is almost universally held in critical scholarship.

[61] Psalms 110 is considered by many futurists as the definitive text to prove a future coming of the Lord. However, see my book on the parable of the Nobleman in Luke 19 for an in–depth refutation of that claim. The connection between Isaiah 25–>Matthew 8—> 1 Corinthians 15 alone shows that the time of Abraham sitting at the Resurrection Banquet was in AD 70.

Notice the argument:

The time of the Banquet of Isaiah 25 (the time of Matthew 8:11) is the time of the resurrection of 1 Corinthians 15:55–56.

The time of the resurrection of 1 Corinthians 15 (the resurrection of Isaiah 25) is the time when "the last enemy" ("the death") would be put down for those in Christ (1 Corinthians 15:22)—*in fulfillment of Psalms 110.*

Therefore, the time of the Banquet of Isaiah 25 (the time of Matthew 8:11) is the time when "the last enemy" ("the death") would be put down for those in Christ (1 Corinthians 15:22) in fulfillment of Psalms 110.

Following on that, consider the following:

The time of the Banquet of Isaiah 25 (the time of Matthew 8:11) is the time when "the last enemy" ("the death") would be put down for those in Christ (1 Corinthians 15:22) in fulfillment of Psalms 110.

But, the time of the Banquet of Isaiah 25 (the time of Matthew 8:11) is the time of the judgment of Old Covenant Israel for violating the everlasting covenant, when "the sons of the kingdom" would be cast out (Isaiah 24:1–5/Matthew 8:11).

Therefore, the time of the fulfillment of Psalms 110, when the "last enemy" was put down, was the time of the Banquet of Isaiah 25 (the time of Matthew 8:11) at the time of the

judgment of Old Covenant Israel for violating the everlasting covenant, and when "the sons of the kingdom" would be cast out (Isaiah 24:1–5/Matthew 8:11)—AD 70.

Let me make an incredibly important point. If Abraham, Isaac, Jacob, the martyrs of Hebrews 11, and the prophets received their kingdom reward through the resurrection to eternal life in AD 70 (in heaven)—as posited by the Dominionists—then clearly, that resurrection to eternal life *did not involve the raising, restoration, and resuscitation of their long–decayed biological bodies.* They patently did not come out of the literal dirt. And if this is true, if they received their resurrection to eternal kingdom life in AD 70, *without being raised out of the dirt of the earth*, then clearly, those entering Christ today do not have to be raised out of dirt to receive eternal life in the kingdom. This is devastating to all futurist views of eschatology. (I should point out that I have made this point numerous times in discussions and have yet to have one person offer any substantive response. The most common response has been ridicule and name–calling, none of which answers the argument).

Former preterist Sam Frost and others, feeling the force of this argument, now claim that Abraham and all the faithful Worthies went directly to heaven when they died and that they are sitting at the Banquet of Matthew 8 awaiting the bodily resurrection.[62] This flies in the face of numerous facts:

#1 ✓ Jesus' emphatic statement while he was still on earth: "No man has ascended to the Father" (John 3:13).

---

[62] This is the view found in the Westminster Confession of Faith, Chapter 8:6.

#2- *V* Peter's declaration on Pentecost that, "David has not ascended into the heavens" (Acts 2:29f).

#3 *V* It violates Hebrews 6:19f that tells us Jesus was the *forerunner* into heaven, the Most Holy Place. The word *forerunner* is from *prodromos* (πρόδρομος, *prodromos, Strong's #4274)*. The word means, "a precursor, an advance guard," it refers to one who goes before, one who leads the way. (See any of the Lexicons). But, according to the view that Abraham and all the OT worthies went to heaven when they died, THEY were the forerunners *that led the way for Jesus!* This is patently false.

#4 *V* It violates Hebrews 9 that clearly teaches that as long as the Old Covenant Cultus—and covenant—stood valid, there was no entrance into the Most Holy Place, i.e. heaven.[63]

#5 *V* It violates Hebrews 11:39–40 which discusses all of the OT Worthies and how they had not entered into the promises made to

---

[63] Hebrews 9:6–10 is an incredibly important eschatological text. In numerous debates I have asked my Amillennial opponents to say where the faithful Christian goes when they die today. I asked Prof. David Hester, (Faulkner University, Montgomery, Alabama) in formal public debate, (2016), this question he said Abraham's bosom in Hades. When I noted that Torah would remain valid, meaning no forgiveness available, as the barrier to entrance into heaven, Hester experienced a "mid–debate conversion," and suddenly affirmed that we have, after all, the full benefit of Christ's atonement! I then pointed out that this demands that Christ has come, bringing salvation. He refused to discuss the issue further. A book of that debate is available on my websites, Amazon, Kindle and other retailers.

them, which included "the better resurrection" (11:35). So, when Hebrews was written, Abraham, Isaac, and all the Worthies had not received the resurrection. But Matthew 8:11 depicts Abraham and the Worthies receiving the resurrection promise by sitting at the Resurrection Banquet promised in Isaiah 25. Thus, if Abraham and the Worthies had actually sat down at the Resurrection Banquet centuries, millennia, before Christ, (per the Westminster Confession and other commentators) then they had in fact entered into resurrection life. Since Hebrews 11 shows that Abraham and all the OT Worthies had not entered into resurrection—eternal life—when that book was written, it is clearly wrong to say that those Worthies went to heaven, entering into their hope, long before Hebrews was written.

#6 V It violates Revelation 11 & 15 that show that there could be no entrance into heaven, i.e. The Most Holy Place, until the judgment of Babylon—Old Covenant Jerusalem.

Very clearly, no man entered heaven prior to the finished work of Christ. And thus, the Westminster Confession and those who claim that all of the faithful Worthies who died prior to the finished work of Christ entered heaven, are simply wrong.

I think Martin Luther expressed it well in addressing the idea that all the OT worthies went to heaven prior to the work of Christ. As for the popular notion that the souls of the righteous have the full enjoyment of heaven prior to the resurrection, Luther whimsically remarked, "It would take a foolish soul to desire its body when it was already in heaven!"[64]

---

[64] D. Martin Luthers Werke, ed. Tischreden (Weimar, 1912–1921), p.5534, cited by Althaus, op. cit, p.417.

In addition to all of this, sitting at the Banquet in Matthew 8 and the parallel of Luke 13:28f would take place, "when the sons of the kingdom are cast out." But according to Frost, the casting out of the sons of the kingdom and sitting down at the resurrection Banquet were totally unrelated temporally, even though Jesus' words are explicit and emphatic:

> There will be weeping and gnashing of teeth, when you see Abraham and Isaac and Jacob and all the prophets in the kingdom of God, and yourselves thrust out. They will come from the east and the west, from the north and the south, and sit down in the kingdom of God (Luke 13:28–29).

Notice the antecedent to "*they* will come from the east and the west." It is Abraham, Isaac, and Jacob! "They" would come from the east and west and sit down—with others—at the Banquet—and that would be when "you yourselves" were cast out. Words could hardly be clearer. Abraham and the Worthies would not sit at the Banquet table *until the resurrection*. How could they, if Isaiah was predicting the yet future to him establishment of the Messianic Resurrection Banquet? If that Banquet was future to Isaiah, then it was not a reality in the days of Abraham.

Now, the idea of a physical resurrection of human corpses out of the ground at the end of time, is so entrenched in the tradition and history of the church that I well recognize how challenging the former comments are.[65] I certainly was not raised understanding what I have just written. I ask, however, that you consider them carefully. And to close this discussion let me offer some ever so brief thoughts to hopefully challenge your thinking further. I want to challenge your thinking in regard to the idea of a physical resurrection.

I have engaged numerous debate opponents all of whom have insisted that the resurrection is an "end of time" event when "the last enemy"[66] i.e. *physical death* is abolished. They have affirmed that "the death" that entered the day Adam sinned was in physical death, and that physical death remains today as "the wages of sin."

It must be kept in mind that the very foundation of futurism is the idea that Adamic Death, the death that is the "wages of sin" is physical

---

[65] For an in–depth study of the resurrection and the "destruction of the Death of Adam" see my book, *The Death of Adam/The Life of Christ*. (Ardmore, Ok; JaDon Management Inc. 2019). Available from my websites, Amazon, Kindle and other retailers.

[66] One of the questions that I constantly pose to my opponents is: "Is physical death the enemy of the child of God, redeemed and forgiven?" Amazingly, virtually all futurists say "Yes." I have then asked, if it is true that physical death ushers the saint into the presence of God in heaven, where they enjoy fellowship with the savior and all the wonderful faithful of the ages, just exactly how and why is our death, our enemy? According to Hebrews, the hope of the Christian is entrance into heaven. So, once again, if the Christian enters into heaven when we die, receiving the fulfillment of our hope, just exactly how is our death our enemy? I have not had one single person give any kind of substantive answer. See my *Death of Adam/Life of Christ* book in which I discuss this issue in depth.

death. This is *the* foundation of all futurist views of the resurrection. So, the death that entered through Adam's sin is *physical death*, and, the wages of sin is *physical death*. Keep this in mind.

Please consider that Paul said that Christ was "the first to be raised from the dead" (Acts 26:21f). He also said that Christ was the "first fruit" of the resurrection harvest (1 Corinthians 15:19f), the firstborn of (out from) the dead (Colossians 1:18f). To say that this is problematic for the futurist views of resurrection and the definition of Adamic Death is an understatement. Here is why.

Paul unequivocally taught that deliverance from the Adamic Death Curse—physical death, per futurism—is resurrection *to eternal life*, immortality. This is undeniable in 1 Corinthians 15:55–56:

> So when this corruptible has put on incorruption, and this mortal has put on immortality, then shall be brought to pass the saying that is written: "Death is swallowed up in victory." "O Death, where is your sting? O Hades, where is your victory?"[67]

Keep in mind that the traditional view of *corruption* in this text is that it refers to the human body destined to die physically as a direct result of Adam's sin and our own. Thus, since physical death is "the Curse of Adam" then when the human body is raised from the physical death in resurrection that *is* the change from mortality to immortality, from

---

[67] Please pay particular attention to the fact that Paul quotes from Isaiah 25:6–8 as we have already noted. Thus, Paul was anticipating the Resurrection Banquet. Abraham and the Worthies had clearly NOT already sat down at that Banquet table when Paul wrote.

corruption to incorruption. That is—no matter what else one may claim—deliverance from the wages of sin.

To put it another way, physical death is (supposedly) the Adamic Curse (the curse of mortality). Resurrection from physical death, we are told, is deliverance from mortality—the Adamic Curse. This is critical: In Paul's resurrection theology, *there is no resurrection for the saints that is NOT resurrection to immortality and eternal life.*

So, again, at the risk of redundancy, to be resurrected is to be delivered from the Adamic Death Curse and receive immortality and eternal life. That is Paul's resurrection doctrine.

Consider now, more closely, Paul's statement that Christ was "the first to be raised from the dead"; that he was the "first fruit" of the resurrection harvest and that he was the first born of the dead (Colossians 1:18).[68]

And yet, please catch the power of this:

---

[68] Notice that Paul says Christ was the first born "out from the dead" (*ek ton nekron*). Now, were all of those who died prior to Christ "the dead ones"? Of course. And were not those who were raised from physical death prior to Jesus' resurrection not raised "out from" physical death? Clearly so. Thus, once again, if physical death is the key focus, then Paul was clearly wrong to say that Christ was the first to be raised "out from the dead." Something beyond and different from physical death is in play here.

158

Many people were raised out of physical death before Jesus was raised from physical death.[69]
(Do you see the insurmountable problem here?)

To be resurrected from physical death is to be delivered from the Adamic Death Curse, delivered from the wages of sin, to be free from the law of sin and death and receive immortality and eternal life.

Therefore, those raised from physical death (the Adamic Death Curse) *before Jesus was raised from physical death,* **were raised to eternal life and immortality.**

We have proven that resurrection, in Paul's theology was deliverance from Adamic Death. Since the futurist position is that physical death *is* the Adamic Death (the wages of sin), then it is specious to speak of saints[70]—those raised before Christ—being raised out of physical death to any other kind of life than eternal life and immortality! Yet, this is precisely what the futurists do.

---

[69] Elijah raised the son of the Zarephath widow (1 Kings 17:17–22). Elisha raised the son of the Shunammite woman (2 Kings 4:32–35). A man was raised from the dead when his body touched Elisha's bones (2 Kings 13:20, 21). The daughter of the Widow Nain was raised—before Christ (Luke 7:11f). Jairus' daughter was raised out from the dead before Christ (Luke 8:41, 42, 49–55). Lazarus was raised out from the dead—before Christ.

[70] In 1 Corinthians 15 Paul never discusses the resurrection of the wicked. Many commentators have noted this.

159

For instance, Simon Kistemaker actually claims that:

> Christ is not the first fruit of those who have been
> raised out of those who died. In fact, no human being
> has been raised physically from the dead. The sons of
> both the widow of Zeraphath and the Shunammite
> died in later years; so did the daughters of Jairus, the
> young man of Nain, and Lazarus. Only Christ has
> conquered death and risen from the dead. All the
> others must wait for their bodily resurrection until the
> appointed time. (p. 551)—"But each in his own
> order; Christ the first fruits." , Paul uses the word
> *tagma*, which in other places relates to companies of
> soldiers; here, it is devoid of any connection with the
> military. It means first "rank" and next "order.":
> Christ is the first born from among those raised from
> the dead and has supremacy (Colossians 1:18): he is
> also the first in sequence. After Christ has been
> raised, then those who belong to him will receive a
> glorified body. Christ the first in the resurrection
> will be followed by countless multitudes who belong
> to him.[71]

Kistemaker realizes that if physical death is the definition of Adamic
Death that Jesus was clearly NOT the first person to be raised out of
physical death—as Paul affirms so clearly. So, he redefines
resurrection as not simply being delivered out of physical death, but,
being raised to die no more. Since, says he, all those raised out from
the dead prior to Christ died again, then they were not truly
resurrected! But Paul knows nothing of such a distinction. There

---

[71] Simon Kistemaker, *New Testament Commentary*,
(Grand Rapids; Baker Academic, 1993), 548.

was only ONE Adamic Death, and "the resurrection" was deliverance from that death. If therefore physical death is "the death" of Adam, then quite simply, to be delivered from physical death is to receive eternal life. There is no escaping this. We have every right to ask: How is it possible to define Adamic Death as physical death, and yet then say that to be raised out of physical death is not truly resurrection and it is not deliverance from the Adamic Curse? That smacks of double talk.

As seen, when it is noted that Paul said Christ was the first to be raised from the dead, the firstborn of the dead, the first fruit of the resurrection *harvest,* the "answer" is given that Christ was not the first person to be raised from physical death, but he was the first to be raised to die no more. He was the first to be raised to eternal life. But, that flies in the face of futurists' definition of Adamic Death, the wages of sin as physical death. When it is argued, as virtually all futurists do, that physical death itself *IS* the Adamic Curse, and it *IS* the wages of sin, it is logically specious to say that one could be raised from physical death without being delivered from Adamic Death and delivered from the wages of sin.

One final thought. I will not develop it here, but when Paul said Christ was the first fruit of the harvest, this demands that *the resurrection harvest had begun.*[72] There is no escaping this. Yet, many commentators, understanding the implication of "first fruit" nonetheless say that the harvest has not occurred for 2000 years! But if Jesus' physical resurrection was itself the first fruit, then we have every right to ask, has there been—*why has there not been*—an on–going harvest, the raising of human corpses out of the dirt, ever since

---

[72] See my *The Death of Adam/The Life of Christ* where I develop this in detail.

161

Jesus' resurrection? There is simply no exegetical justification for inserting a two millennia gap between the first fruit and the harvest. The empirical reality that there has not been—and there is not now—a harvest of physical bodies coming out of the ground proves that the entire argument about physical resurrection being the focus of Christ's physical resurrection as the first fruit is false.

When it is argued, as virtually all futurists do, that physical death itself *IS* the Adamic Curse, that it *IS* the wages of sin, then it is logically specious to say that one could be raised from physical death without being delivered from Adamic Death and delivered from the wages of sin.

This being true- and it is- then to say that Christ was the first to be raised from the Adamic Death is patently false. *Everyone* that was raised out of physical death before Christ was raised, was delivered from the Adamic Death, delivered from the wages of sin. Thus, they _MUST_ have received eternal life!

The futurist definition of Adamic death is, therefore, completely false.

All of this comports perfectly with our discussion of Matthew 8 above. Abraham and the Worthies were to sit at the *Resurrection Banquet* when the sons of the kingdom were cast out. That was the time of the resurrection. But, the sons of the kingdom, Old Covenant Judah/Israel were cast out in AD 70. Therefore, the Resurrection Banquet was fully established in AD 70 at the end of the Old Covenant age. But, while Abraham and the Worthies entered into the kingdom and eternal life fully at that time, it is more evident— empirically so—that they were not raised in restored, reconstructed, physical bodies that had been raised out of the dirt. Is that not undeniably true?

It is time to realize that the futurist definition of Adamic Death, and the "wages of sin" as physical death is simply wrong.

How Could Jesus Call the Message of the Impending Fall of Jerusalem, the Gospel (the "Good News!") of the Kingdom?

Point # 13

Because the Destruction of the Temple and Cultus Powerfully and Effectively Put an End to the Judaizing Movement

Some might think that this point is anachronistic and therefore inapplicable. Of course, it is to be admitted that when Jesus uttered the words in Matthew 24:14 there was no Judaizing movement within the church. That is undeniable. However, it would be, I suggest, naive to think that Jesus did not know what was coming—he clearly did since the Olivet Discourse is, in fact, his prediction of the coming of false teachers. And make no mistake, false teachers did come, and they did lead away many from the Gospel. One of those chief heresies, a key cause of the apostasy in the early church was the Judaizers.

The pervasive, wide–spread and *devastating* impact of the Judaizing movement in the early church is sometimes overlooked, or perhaps depreciated. But, it was everywhere, and it threatened the very foundation and existence of the Gospel. What was the Judaizing movement? It can be summarized in Acts 15:1–2:

> Certain people came down from Judea to Antioch and were teaching the believers: "Unless you are circumcised, according to the custom taught by Moses, you cannot be saved."

So, the message of the Judaizers was that Jesus was indeed the promised Messiah and that the Gentiles were being called into Israel's promised salvation and kingdom. The salvation of the Gentiles coming to Jerusalem and worshiping the God of Israel was, after all, promised in the Tanakh. However, for the Gentiles to fully enjoy the Messiah's salvation, they had to keep the Law of Moses and be circumcised. If one takes a literalistic approach to many of the OT prophecies concerning the Gentiles it is not too difficult to understand the argument of the Judaizers. After all, as just noted, the Old Covenant did predict that the Gentiles would come to Messiah, but, they had to worship in Zion offer sacrifices and be circumcised. That is, if taken literally, that is what the OT prophecies foretold. Just a few examples will suffice to demonstrate.

*– Isaiah 2:2–4 —

> Now it shall come to pass in the latter days That the mountain of the Lord's house Shall be established on the top of the mountains, And shall be exalted above the hills; And all nations shall flow to it. Many people shall come and say, "Come, and let us go up to the mountain of the Lord, To the house of the God of Jacob; He will teach us His ways, And we shall walk in His paths." For out of Zion shall go forth the law, And the word of the Lord from Jerusalem.

When the Kingdom would be established the Law (ostensibly Torah) would go forth from Jerusalem. Thus, taken in a literalistic sense, the *land of Israel,* and Jerusalem would be the center and the capital of the Kingdom. But there is more here.

* – Isaiah 2:2–4 —Notice that "All the nations,"—Gentiles, not just Israel—would pilgrimage to Jerusalem/Zion. Thus, in a very real sense, the Judaizing message was that the Gentile Christians had to set their minds on "the land," the city and the temple.

165

*— Isaiah 52:1–3 —

> Awake, awake! Put on your strength, O Zion; Put on
> your beautiful garments, O Jerusalem, the holy city!
> For the uncircumcised and the unclean Shall no
> longer come to you. Shake yourself from the dust,
> arise; Sit down, O Jerusalem! Loose yourself from
> the bonds of your neck, O captive daughter of Zion!

I have often thought that this passage, perhaps conflated with Ezekiel
43, was the ground for the claim of the Judaizers that anyone coming
into the Messianic Temple had to be circumcised. The text does,
after all, say that no uncircumcised person would be able to worship
the Lord acceptably. So, interpreted literally and physically, that
made for a powerful supportive text for the Judaizers.

*— Isaiah 56: 1–8 —

> Do not let the son of the foreigner Who has joined
> himself to the Lord Speak, saying, "The Lord has
> utterly separated me from His people"; Nor let the
> eunuch say, "Here I am, a dry tree." For thus says the
> Lord: "To the eunuchs who keep My Sabbaths, And
> choose what pleases Me, And hold fast My covenant,
> Even to them I will give in My house And within My
> walls a place and a name Better than that of sons and
> daughters; I will give them an everlasting name That
> shall not be cut off. Also the sons of the foreigner
> Who join themselves to the Lord, to serve Him, And
> to love the name of the Lord, to be His servants—
> Everyone who keeps from defiling the Sabbath, And
> holds fast My covenant Even them I will bring to My

166

holy mountain, And make them joyful in My house of prayer. Their burnt offerings and their sacrifices Will be accepted on My altar; For My house shall be called a house of prayer for all nations." The Lord God, who gathers the outcasts of Israel, says, "Yet I will gather to him Others besides those who are gathered to him."

In this marvelous text we find the promise of the conversion of those previously excluded from the Temple and the cultus. Both those physically blemished and the foreigner (those not of the tribes, not of the lineage of Israel) would be welcomed. They would be given a name better than sons and daughters!

They would not only be welcomed into the Messianic Temple, but they could offer up acceptable sacrifices, "burnt offerings" to the Lord. (See also Isaiah 60 where the Gentiles would ascend the altar of the Lord to make acceptable sacrifices). This is *stunning*, if taken in any kind of a literalistic manner. Foreigners offering sacrifices, burnt offers on the altar in the temple? This was a radical—revolutionary—concept and thought.

Not only would those previously excluded be welcomed, the eunuch and the foreigner would be members of the covenant community and observe the Sabbath.

Personally, I see that Paul, in Colossians 2, was responding directly to the Judaizers who were employing passages such as Isaiah 52 and 56. More on this below.

Notice what Paul argues in Colossians 2:11–17:

> In Him you were also circumcised with the
> circumcision made without hands, by putting off the
> body of the sins of the flesh, by the circumcision of
> Christ, buried with Him in baptism, in which you also
> were raised with Him through faith in the working of
> God, who raised Him from the dead. And you, being
> dead in your trespasses and the uncircumcision of
> your flesh, He has made alive together with Him,
> having forgiven you all trespasses, having wiped out
> the handwriting of requirements that was against us,
> which was contrary to us. And He has taken it out of
> the way, having nailed it to the cross. Having
> disarmed principalities and powers, He made a public
> spectacle of them, triumphing over them in it. So let
> no one judge you in food or in drink, or regarding a
> festival or a new moon or Sabbaths,

The Judaizers were saying that Gentiles had to be physically
circumcised to be members of the New Creation. Paul said that the
Gentiles had been circumcised, *in their hearts, by faith.*

The Judaizers were saying that Gentiles had to be circumcised to be
saved. Paul said the Gentiles had been buried with Christ in baptism,
raised by faith in the operation of God. They had been dead, now they
were alive.[73]

---

[73] Paul's affirmation of the "resurrection" of the
Colossians should not be missed. They had been dead in their
sins. But, they had been buried with Christ in baptism. By faith
in the Lord, they had been raised from baptism to life. That is

The Judaizers were saying that the Gentiles had to set their affection on "the earth" i.e. "The *land*" (Jerusalem—where the cultus was centered[74]) and observe the festal mandates of Torah, that restricted the eating of meats, that commanded observance of "New Moons, feast days and Sabbaths."

Clearly, the Judaizers were telling the Gentile Christians that they had to observe the "New Moons, feast days and the Sabbaths." It cannot be overlooked that to observe those feast days, pilgrimage to Jerusalem was necessary. So, by telling the Gentiles that they had to observe the feast days, that logically demands that the Gentiles were being told that they had to keep the Law of Moses in regard to the pilgrimages to Jerusalem (Exodus 34:23). They had to set their affection, their minds, on the land.

So, it appears that everything foretold by Isaiah 52 and 56 (and other prophecies) when taken *literally*, was being imposed on the Gentiles

---

resurrection language that should not be dismissed. See Paul's similar resurrection teaching in Romans 6. Paul's discussion falsifies the claim that in the Bible that only kind of death that is discussed is physical death (e.g. former preterist Sam Frost makes this utterly disingenuous claim). But Paul said the Colossians had been—past tense—D-E-A-D, but were now alive.

[74] See my book, *Minds MisPlaced: Colossians 3:1–2 and Dispensationalism*, in which I show that Paul's paranesis: "do not place your affections on the earth" (Colossians 3:1–3) should be rendered "do not set your affections on *the land*." *Everything* that Paul was telling the Gentiles that they did not have to observe and should not be judged on, was centered in "the land." (Ardmore, Ok; JaDon Management, 2018)

by the Judaizers. They seemingly had a great Biblical argument. Not only that, but the continuing existence and practice of the Jerusalem cultus was, in the mind of the Judaizers, proof positive that God intended for the Gentiles to obey the God of Israel just as they did— by submission to the Law of Moses. Paul would have nothing of this, and the Jerusalem Council rejected this claim (Acts 15). But, that did not prevent the widespread contagion of the Judaizers from spreading. In fact, the Judaizing movement appears on the pages of virtually every NT epistle.

We have already seen how it sprang up in Acts 15.

In the epistle to the Romans, Paul had to deal with those very Jew/Gentile issues, the eating of meats sacrificed to idols. He told the Romans: "The kingdom is not in meats and drinks" (Romans 14:17f). He was addressing the Judaizers who were imposing Torah and the cultus, which did stand "in meats, drinks, and different ordinances" (Hebrews 9:8f).

In Corinthians , both epistles, he likewise had to address the issue of eating of meats and circumcision (1 Corinthians 7–8; 10, etc).

In Galatians, the Judaizing movement was so strong that Paul marveled that the Galatian churches had so soon departed from the Gospel.

In Colossians 2 he had to urge the brethren not to be deprived of their salvation by those who would try to "synagogue them"[75] In

---

[75] In a highly suggestive comment on Colossians 2:8,
N. T. Wright says: "In other words (v. 8) don't let anyone
lead you away captive. But the word Paul uses for 'lead away

170

verses 14f he told the Gentile brethren not to be "judged" on their observance, or non–observance, of "the New Moons, feast days and Sabbaths." He reminded them that the elements (the *stoichea*) of that cultic world were passing away:

> Therefore, if you died with Christ from the basic principles of the world, why, as though living in the world, do you subject yourselves to regulations— "Do not touch, do not taste, do not handle," which all concern things which perish with the using— according to the commandments and doctrines of men? (Colossians 2:20–21)

Nothing could better epitomize the Jerusalem cultus, the Mosaic laws and festival ordinances than these verses. And Paul reminded them that those cultic practices were mere shadows of the "good things about to come" (v. 16). Those cultic practices and laws were the "elements of the world" that Paul (and Peter in 2 Peter 3) referred to as the elements and the world that was in the very process of passing when he wrote.

He was not talking about "earth, wind, fire, and water," considered as the "elements" of material creation. After all, he said the Colossian brethren were no longer enslaved by and to those

---

captive', the very rare word sylagogon: ὁ συλαγωγῶν..., seems, like the equivalent words in Philippians 3, to be a contemptuous pun. All you have to do is invert the lambda (in cursive writing) or add a stroke to it (in capitals) and you get synagogon: συναγωγῶν; in other words, 'don't let anyone en–synagogue you, drag you into the synagogue.'" (N. T. Wright, *Paul*, (Minneapolis, Fortress, 2005)117). Given the entire context of Colossians 2, I believe this comment has great merit.

elements. So, if he was talking about the physical elements of material creation, are we to believe that Paul was saying that the Colossians were no longer subject to the laws of nature?? That is patently untenable.[76] I am confident that after they became Christians they were still subject to gravity, to heat, to hunger, to thirst, to high winds, to fire!

So, what we have in Colossians is Paul arguing against the Judaizers, urging the Gentile Christians not to be deprived of their salvation by submitting to Torah and the cultus, because Torah and the cultus was about to pass away! Paul was pointing to the impending end and destruction of the Temple and the cultus as a definitive refutation of the Judaizing doctrine. He was saying that it was necessary for that Old Covenant world to pass away for the "good things" to be fully realized. This is, in a nutshell, *the Gospel of Destruction!* The end of that Old Covenant world, with the dissolution of the temple and cultus, was to be the ultimate, dramatic, powerful and definitive refutation of the Judaizers.[77]

So, this discussion, while somewhat brief, nonetheless shows that the impending destruction of Jerusalem was surely a "good news" "bad

---

[76] In discussing the "elements of the world" in Colossians 2, Scott McKnight examines the various definitions given to define them. He concludes that Paul was referring to the basic doctrines of Torah and the cultus. (Scott McKnight, *Colossians, International Commentary on the New Testament,* (Grand Rapids; Eerdmans, 2018), 226+).

[77] We could discuss Timothy, Hebrews, Peter, and Revelation in this discussion since those epistles clearly contain polemic against the Judaizers. But for brevity I will not include those discussions here.

news" message. To reiterate, on the physical level, that event was horrific beyond description. On the other hand, for the early church struggling with and against the Judaizing movement, that event signaled in a powerful and undeniable way that the land, the city, the temple, and the cultus was now wiped away. Jesus, Messiah, the King, had himself come in judgment of that Old Covenant world. He had foretold its destruction and his disciples repeated that message for a generation. When that prophecy came to pass, it vindicated Christ as the Son of God, revealing him to be "King of kings and Lord of lords" and in so doing, vindicated the suffering of his disciples. That horrendous event shattered any and all appeals and messages that said "Look, the temple, the cultus, the priesthood remains. This is God's will for you!"

No, the message of the end of that Old Covenant age truly was "the *Gospel* of the Kingdom." The *Gospel of Destruction* was truly a wonderful message when viewed in this light and context.

Point # 14

Restoring the Good News of the Kingdom;
The Gospel of Destruction?

If what I have presented above is true, and I am convinced that it is, it raises a very serious question: How is it, *why* is it, that an understanding of the importance of the fall of Jerusalem has seemingly been lost. There can be little doubt that in modern, evangelical Christianity, the significance of that event is virtually unknown. In fact, when the destruction of Jerusalem is introduced into discussions of eschatology, the response very often is, "What does that have to do with anything?"

In several formal public debates, my opponents have literally scoffed at the idea that the destruction of the temple and Jerusalem had any spiritual significance. For instance, John Welch, minister in the churches of Christ made this argument in our 2008 formal public debate in Indianapolis. Why, he asked, would the folks in Athens, Corinth, Thessalonica, etc., who lived "hundreds of miles" from Jerusalem, care about the destruction of the outpost city of Jerusalem?

I responded to Welch (and others) by noting that if the fall of Temple and City at the end of the Old Covenant age was insignificant and meaningless to folks living hundreds of miles away, then surely, the death of Jesus, who was, according to leading "authorities" of the day a blasphemer, a heretic, a fake and charlatan, even less significant! I mean, after all, he was just one of three miscreants that died on that Golgatha hill that day! Not only that, Jesus' death was hundreds of miles from those cities and was *thousands of miles from the USA*! When I made this argument in response to Welch there was a visible shock wave that went through the audience, and Welch never answered my argument.

The reality is that the "size" of an event does not determine its importance. That temple symbolized the Old Covenant age of Moses and the law. Thus, when both the OT and the New posit the end of that Old Covenant age at the disaster that was AD 70, then to suggest that that event was meaningless is specious. The historical reality is that the fall of Jerusalem was perceived to be of far, far more importance than the death of just another rabble–rousing Jew. Would those who devalue the importance of AD 70, say that it was more important than the death of Jesus? More people knew about the destruction of Jerusalem—and celebrated it—with Roman Triumph marches and the Arch of Titus. Roman historians wrote of the great triumph over Jerusalem—none did that with the death of Jesus.

The fall of Jerusalem and the end of the Old Covenant age was necessary for salvation to go fully to the Gentiles, manifesting that the days of God's dealing with one exclusive people were over. The fall of Jerusalem put an end to the Judaizing movement. Their claim that a person had to keep the law of Moses and be circumcised to be saved (Acts 15) was now moot and empty. They could no longer point to Jerusalem and the Temple cultus as proof that God demanded all men to serve Him in and through that Temple and priesthood. Thus, Paul told his Gentile audience, being pressured into conformity to Torah, that the "*elements* of the world" (Elements is from στοιχείων, stoicheiôn, Strong's #4747) the very fabric of Old Covenant Israel, was passing away. Therefore, they were not to put their confidence on "the land" but on Christ, the reality to which that Old Cultus pointed (Colossians 2:14f).

Note, when Paul said do not put your affections on the *earth*, as the great majority of translations render it, I believe that this misses something very important in the context. Paul is urging his Gentile audience not to engage in the Temple ordinances, the "New Moons, Feast Days and Sabbath." Those festal praxes were shadows of the

175

good things about to come. My point is that when Paul steered them away from the cultus, he was also likewise urging them not to put their attention, love and focus on the "Promised Land." The word translated as earth, is from *ge*, and can be translated as land or earth. In the context of Colossians 2–3, the debate is over the abiding validity of Torah, of Temple, of feast days—and by logical extension—on *the Land of Israel*! The focus is not on the globe, but on the land where the "new moons, feast days and Sabbath" were centralized.[78]

As suggested above, for literally centuries the historical church has lost, or abandoned, the reality of the importance of the fall of Jerusalem in AD 70. In our discussion in this work I hope the reader can begin to recapture some sense of why that event is so important to understand. As R. C. Sproul expresssed it:

> No matter what view of eschatology we embrace, we must take seriously the redemptive–historical importance of Jerusalem's destruction in A.D.70.[79]

Even though Sproul maintained a futurist eschatology, nonetheless, for daring to point out the incredible significance of the fall of Jerusalem, he was castigated in his own circles for giving "ammunition" to the "heretical" full preterist paradigm.

---

[78] See my book, *Misplaced Minds: A Refutation of Zionism and Dispensationalism* for a full discussion of this. The book is available from my websites, Amazon, Kindle and other retailers.

[79] R. C. Sproul, *The Last Days According to Jesus,* (Grand Rapids; Baker Books, 2000), 26.

There are many factors that have contributed to this that we cannot discuss here. But, the loss of the sense of the importance of that awful catastrophe has undoubtedly been lost. The end of the Old Covenant age has been posited at the Cross instead of at the destruction of the Temple, where the disciples clearly posited it in Matthew 24:3. But lamentably, the majority view in Christianity today is that the disciples were misguided, ignorant or confused to conflate the end of the age with the fall of the Temple. The trouble is, those disciples of Jesus were not the ones confused on that day. It is the modern commentators who are confused and who refuse to see the eschatological significance of the end of the Old Covenant age. By divorcing Biblical eschatology from the end of Israel's covenant age, historical Christianity has completely missed the Biblical narrative of the end–times.

It is important for the reader to see, however, that in earlier times, many church leaders and even "pagans" have recognized the incredible importance of that world changing event.

Eusebius Pamphilius—early fourth century—(Not Eusebius of Caesarea) in his "lost" work Theophania (circa 310 A.D.), translated by Samuel Lee (1843) recognized that in the fall of Jerusalem, Jesus came:

> All authorities concur in the declaration that "when all these things should have been done" "The End" should come: that "the mystery of God should be finished as he had declared to His servants the prophets": it should be completed: time should now be no more: the End of all things (so foretold) should be at hand, and be fully brought to pass: in these days should be fulfilled all that had been spoken of Christ (and of His church) by the prophets: or, **in**

177

other words, when the gospel should have been preached in all the world for a testimony to all nations, and the power of the Holy People be scattered (abroad), then should the End come, then should all these things be finished. I need now only say, all these things have been done: the old and elementary system passed away with a great noise; all these predicted empires have actually fallen, and the new kingdom, the new heaven and earth, the new Jerusalem—all of which were to descend from God, to be formed by His power, have been realized on earth; all these things have been done in the sight of all the nations; God's holy arm has been made bare in their sight: His judgments have prevailed, and they remain for an everlasting testimony to the whole world. His kingdom has come, as it was foretold it should, and His will has, so far, been done; His purposes have been finished; and, from that day to the extreme end of time, it will be the duty, as indeed it will be the great privilege of the Church, to gather into its bosom the Jew, the Greek, the Scythian, the Barbarian, bond and free; and to do this as the Apostles did in their days—in obedience, faith and hope.[80] (My emphasis).

Similarly, Eusebius of Caesarea, commonly called the Father of Church History, believed that the Lord came in AD 70, in fulfillment of OT prophecies. Commenting on Micah 1:2–4; 3:9–12; 4:1–4 said that the Lord *came* in the fall of Jerusalem in A.D. 70. He says that the

---

80

http://www.preteristarchive.com/ChurchHistory/0310_eusebiu s_theophania.html—my emphasis.

time when men would not take up sword against one another anymore, when every man would, "have his own fig tree, according to the prophecy" (Micah 4:1–4), had been realized. He quotes verbatim the prophecy of the coming of the Lord out of heaven as predicted in Micah 1:2–4, and says this occurred with the fall of Jerusalem.[81] Citing Micah's prophecy that Jerusalem would be plowed like a field, he says he had seen that with his own eyes.

Likewise, commenting on Zechariah 14 and the prediction of the coming of the Lord with all of His saints and the siege and destruction of the city, he says "the present prophecy foretells a second siege of Jerusalem which is to take place afterwards, which it suffered from the Romans, after its inhabitants carried through their outrage on our Savior Jesus Christ. Thus, the coming of our Savior and the events connected therewith are very clearly shewn in this passage—I mean what was done at the time of His Passion, and the siege that came on the Hebrew race directly after, the taking of Jerusalem, the call of the Gentiles also, and the knowledge attained by all nations of the one and only God." (*Proof*, Book VI, Ch. 18, 26).

Eusebius also said that *Christ came,* "with the chariots and horses" to conquer the army of the Jews. He pointed to the destruction of Jerusalem as proof positive of the coming of the Lord as a past event—not a yet future event!

> When, then, we see what was of old foretold for the nations fulfilled in our own day, and when the lamentation and wailing that was predicted for the Jews, and the burning of the Temple and its utter destruction, can also be seen even now to have

---

[81] *Proof of the Gospel*, Bk. VIII, chapter 3, 140+.

occurred according to the prediction, surely we must also agree that the King who was prophesied, the Christ of God, has come, since the signs of His coming have been shewn in each instance I have treated to have been clearly fulfilled (Proof, Bk. VIII, 4, 147).

We can also show that this historian posited the end of the Law of Moses at the fall of Jerusalem:

> Moses himself foresaw by the Holy Spirit that when the New covenant was revived by Christ and preached to all nations, his own legislation would become superfluous, he rightly confined its influence to one place, so that if they were ever deprived of it and shut out of that national freedom, it might not be possible for them to carry out the ordinances of his law in a foreign country, and of necessity they would have to receive the new covenant announced by Christ. Moses had foretold this very thing and in due course Christ sojourned in this life, and the teaching of the new covenant was borne to all nations, and at once the Romans besieged Jerusalem and destroyed it and the Temple there. At once the whole of the Mosaic law was abolished, with all that remained of the Old Covenant, and the curse passed over to those who became lawbreakers because they obeyed Moses' law, when its time had gone by, and still clung ardently to it, for at that very moment, the perfect teaching of the new Law was introduced in its place (*Proof*, 1981, 34–35).

As I document in my book, *We Shall Meet Him In The Air, the Wedding of the King of kings*, (Noted earlier) many (if not most) of the early writers, while they were still clearly futurists, nonetheless pointed to the fall of Jerusalem as an unparalleled event with incredible spiritual significance.

When I say that those early church writers were clearly futurists, one has a perfect right to ponder how, in light of their comments about the coming of the Lord in AD 70, they could continue to believe in a future coming of the Lord. They *knew* that AD 70 was the end of the age. They *knew* that the Lord came in AD 70. They *knew* that the Old Law passed away at that very time. They *knew* that the OT prophecies of the coming of the Lord in judgment were fulfilled at that time— including Daniel 9 and the seventy weeks. They *knew* that the Old Heaven and Earth passed at that time. They *knew* that the Abomination of Desolation and the Great Tribulation were fulfilled in those auspicious days. In short, it can be shown that many—if not most—of the early church "authorities" believed that virtually every major eschatological tenet was fulfilled in AD 70. How then, did they look beyond that event to another end of the age, to another coming of the Lord radically different from AD 70, another New Creation, etc.?

Not only did many of the early writers recognize the importance of the end of the Old Covenant age, but, the enemies of Christ likewise realized the polemic and evangelistic power of the fulfillment of Jesus' prophecy of that event. The fourth–century Roman Emperor Julian, (361–363 C.E.) who came be known as Julian the Apostate by the Christian community, was raised as a Christian. However, he rejected those convictions and became a zealous worshiper of the traditional Roman pantheon of gods and goddesses. He became once again a pagan and antagonistic toward Christianity. He knew, better than most today, how effective and powerful the message of the fulfillment of Jesus' prophecies was in converting both pagans and

Jews. He grew up knowing that Christians pointed to AD 70 as proof positive that Jesus was the Son of God, a true prophet of God. The ruins of the city and temple stood as a continuing powerful proof of their claims.

Julian decided to put the entire power and force of the Roman empire behind the efforts to rebuild the temple. But, in a strange series of events, he was prevented from doing so. Here is one brief description (slightly edited) of those times:

> In Ammianus Marcellinus, Julian is said to have wanted to found the Temple as a memorial to his rule. He arranged for money and building materials to be provided, appointing Alypius of Antioch, but after several attempts to build on the site he was discouraged by a fire which broke out in the ruins there (Res Gestae 23:2–3). The Church Fathers embellished the story in various ways adding that the Jews received Julian's proposal enthusiastically, coming in thousands to the Temple Mount with stones in their hands, but when the first stones were laid the Jews were threatened by earthquakes and hurricanes, and finally driven off by a heavenly fire and specter of Christ (Gregory of Nazianz, Contra Julianum, Oratio, no. 4, 2:149–50; Socrates, Historia Ecclesiastica, 3:196; Sozomenus, Historia Ecclesiastica, 5:214–5). Two important facts may be gathered from these sources: (1) Julian wished to rebuild the Temple to strengthen paganism against Christianity (he saw Judaism and paganism as having sacrificial rites in common); (2) he wished to refute Jesus' prophecy concerning the Temple (Luke 21:6; Matt. 24:2) A Hebrew inscription quoting part of

Isaiah 66:14 found on the Western Wall in 1969 has been ascribed to this period of messianic revival.[82]

Another view of those events can be found here:

> Julian defied the Christianization that was the hallmark of his uncle's (Constantine, DKP) rule and issued edicts that favored Roman cults and minimized the influence of Christianity. He even allowed heretics within the Christian world to occupy positions of ecclesiastical power. Julian's policies were meant to weaken the power of the established Church. The Church and history would always remember him as "Julian the Apostate."
>
> Historian Peter Schafer states that Julian's "attitude to Judaism was ambivalent." The emperor rejected Judaism as the foundation of the Christianity he despised and he did not consider Jews God's chosen people. But the promotion of Judaism and the rebuilding of Jerusalem and the Temple would revive the cult of sacrifice that had long been part of the world while pagans ruled. As well, Julian had hopes of enlisting Jews in the Middle East as allies in his war against the Persians. By 363, the Jews in Jerusalem began to build a third temple. Julian

---

[82] Julian's works were published with an English translation by W.C. Wright under the title *The Works of the Emperor Julian* (3 vols., 1913–23). (https://www.jewishvirtuallibrary.org/julian-the-apostate-x00b 0).

183

composed a letter in Greek to the Jews of the Land of Israel in which, according to historian Jacob R. Marcus, "He abolished the special taxes paid to the Roman government and sought also to stop the payment of tax paid by Jews for the support of the Jewish patriarchate in Palestine. In this same letter he also encouraged the rebuilding of Jerusalem and, we may assume, of the Jewish Temple. Had this attempt been successful it would have meant the reestablishment of the Jewish state with its sacrifices, priests, and more important, its Sanhedrin or Senate."

We have few sources that describe the Jewish response to Julian's startling offer. It seems that Jews from throughout the Diaspora and in the Land of Israel were indeed eager and willing to fulfill their messianic hopes and dreams. Jews attempted to travel to Jerusalem from Babylonia—they were murdered en route by the Persians. But the Christians who dominated Jerusalem would not allow the rebuilding to succeed. Christian sources blame the end of the restoration by claiming a great fire and earthquake destroyed the Temple's foundations, thus proving that Jesus Christ looked upon the Jews with disfavor. These sources are suspect: Most likely the Christians in the city burned down whatever had been constructed. Julian's death in battle in 363 and the end of the pagan experiment in the Christian Roman Empire dashed Jewish hopes for the rebuilding of Jerusalem and the Temple and the return of the Sanhedrin. It is also likely that the rabbinic establishment in the Land of Israel viewed with suspicion the elevation of the kohanim (members of the priestly line) to power in a third temple and were quite ambiguous themselves about Julian's offer. This whole series of events could be reduced to a footnote of history.[83]

The point in this amazing story of Julian's desire and intent to rebuild Jerusalem, and particularly the temple, is that he fully realized the continuing apologetic power of the polemic message conveyed by the ruins of Jerusalem and the Temple. With vigor and conviction the early church pointed to that desolation as proof positive that Jesus was the Son of God. That message resonated in the hearts of pagans and Jews alike—it convinced and convicted them of who Jesus really is. He was no lunatic. He was not a fraud and charlatan. He was no failed prophet. He truly was—he IS—the Son of God!

Jesus himself had said that in the events of the judgment of Jerusalem, they would see, "the sign of the Son of Man in the heavens" (Matthew 24:30). This does not mean, as some believe, that they would see something (even Jesus) appearing in the sky. No, as noted, what the Greek of the text indicates is that the fall of Jerusalem would be the sign that Jesus was (and IS) enthroned as King of kings and Lord of lords! This is precisely how the early church presented the story of Jesus., and they did it with zeal, conviction, power—and effectiveness.

The question is, why doesn't the modern church realize, as the early church did, how important the fall of Jerusalem truly was? I believe there are many reasons:

---

[83]

https://www.jpost.com/Opinion/Emperor-Julian-and-the-dream -of-a-third-temple-516999.

185

.- Loss of an understanding of Hebraic prophetic literature. Which led to the Hellenization of their understanding of Scripture. That meant that they came to expect a literal, bodily, physical coming of Jesus (something scripture never taught) at some proposed end of time.

.- Loss of an understanding of the importance of covenant—and covenant transformation. Modern readers of the Bible normally fail to understand that Israel's covenant with the Lord was the most important reality. Similarly and consequently, they fail to understand the world–changing reality that the end of that covenant world, and the attendant destruction of that Temple that symbolized what that covenant represented.

.- Misunderstanding of the time and nature of God's dealing with Israel. As Romans 11 and other passages show, there arose a belief that God had cut Israel off and that the Gentiles had fully taken their place—all of this prior to the dissolution of the Old Covenant age and the fulfillment of God's promises to Israel.

.- Failure to understand and appreciate that as the previous points note, there was a massive apostasy from the faith in the first century. This is precisely what Jesus foretold (Matthew 24:10–12/Luke 18:1–8), and which did occur. This apostasy, mostly an issue of the Hellenization of the church, led to a loss of understanding of the Hebraic nature of eschatology, of covenant, of the Temple, etc.

.- Failure to understand the importance of "Power and Place" in the ancient world view (See Gregory Stevenson's comment above). The modern world, especially in the West, has lost all sense and appreciation for the incredible importance of Temples in the ancient world. I think Timothy Gray touches on this:

186

The end of the temple and the end of the world are not unrelated events, according to Jewish and early Christian thought. The temple, both in the OT and Second Temple Judaism, symbolized the cosmos. Much of the architecture and artistry employed in the tabernacle and the temple's design point to an embodiment of the cosmos. For instance, the molten washbasin is called "the sea" and the altar, "the bosom of the earth" (1 Kings 7:23–26). The twelve bulls supporting the washbasin were divided into groups of three, each group faced one direction of the compass (1 Kings 7:25, thus signifying the four corners of the world.) The seven lamps on the menorah are referred to as "lights" (Exodus 25:6; 35:8,14,28; 27:20; 39:37; Leviticus 24:2; Numbers 4:9) by the Hebrew word which besides the sanctuary lights is used only in reference to the "lights" spoken of in the fourth day of creation, where the sun, moon, and stars are also called "lights." The seven lights were also seen as representing the five known planets as well as the sun and moon. Josephus and Philo both saw the temple as a symbolic microcosm of the cosmos..... "If Mark recognized the temple as a microcosm of the world, then the end of the temple could not be disassociated from the end of the world—at least not symbolically. Indeed, what better symbol for the end of the world than the demolition of its prototypical representation? This would explain the reference, in the midst of the discourse, about the temple's destruction, to the end of the world. Although these two events seem unrelated to our modern sensibilities, they may well be closely

187

associated within the milieu of first century Judaism."[84]

What is being said here is that in the mind of the first century Jews—including Jesus' apostles in Matthew 24/Mark 13—the destruction of the temple did not mean that literal heaven and earth would be destroyed. It meant that in a very powerful symbolic manner heaven and earth was destroyed!

There may be, and probably are, additional reasons why the modern and historical church has lost the sense of the importance of the fall of Jerusalem. It was far, far more than the destruction of simply the capital of the Jews. It was the "apple of God's eye" for centuries and represented His covenant relationship with them. The destruction of that Temple at the end of the age symbolized that her distinctive and exclusive relationship with the Lord was now at an end. From henceforth, God's salvation was for all men, of all nations—the time has fully come when "neither on this mountain or in Jerusalem shall men worship."

I have tried to share with you just some of the reasons why the destruction of Jerusalem was in fact "the Gospel of Destruction." It was "good news" because it brought to an end the Old Covenant world of sin and death. It was the manifestation of the sons of God. It opened heaven's gates and the gates of God's New Jerusalem to anyone and everyone. Inside this New Jerusalem, we can all find healing. We can find rest. We can find life: "let whosoever will, come!" Amen and Amen!!!

---

[84] Timothy Gray, *The Temple in Mark*, (Grand Rapids; Baker Academic, 2008), 148f.

Index of Scriptures

Exodus
6:6 79
12-14 76
25:6 187
27:20 187
34:23 169
35:8 187
35:14 187
35:28
39:37 187
Leviticus
24:2 187
26 61,107
26:27-33 62,107
Numbers
4:9 187
Deuteronomy
28 61,107
28-30 124
28:49f 62,107
39:15 115
32 57
32:19-27 62,107
32:28 33,57
1 Kings
7:23-26 187
8:27 86
9:1-9 62,107
Psalms
22:31 82
102 49,50,91,118
102:14-28 45,46,
47
102:22 47
110 150,151
113 78
114-118 79
Proverbs
13:12 3
Isaiah
2:2-4 165

5 56
9 108
9:5 108
10 108
10:20f 108
10:21-23 108
11 28,135
11:11-12 135
11:16 135
24 136
24:1-5 146,147,
151,152
24:4-5 146
24:10f 73,146
24-27 32
25 144,146,148,
149,150,151,
154
25-27 74
25-26 55
25:1-6 146,147
25:1-9 53,54,72,
73,144,145,146
25:6-8 22,136,
148,149
25:7 139
25:8 70,139
25:16-19 54,55
26 136
26:9f 119
26:19-21 35,73,74
26:21 58
27 35,36,37,58,
132,133,136
27:1-2 56,74
27:7 136
27:7-8 130
27:9f 132
27:9-13 32,56,74
27:11 33
27:12-13 33,34,

135
27:13 35,58,130,
131,132,133,
133,137,138
43 91
43:5 28
49:6 47
50:3 81
51-54 40
52 37,42,45,167,
169
52:1 39
52:1-3 166
52:1-12 37,38
52:7 40
52:10 41
52:11 41
52:12 39,42
56 47,167,169
56:1-8 166,167
56:1-12 29
59:1-2 136
60 167
61:1-3 46,47
65 20,21,23,24,26,
27,91,119
65:1-2 87
65:8-13 111
65:13 22,119
65:13f 118
65:15-19 111
66 24,26,88,118,
119,122
66:1-2 86,87
66:2-6 87
66:3-5 111
66:9 88
66:14 183
Jeremiah
6:1-8 62,107
7:5-11 117

189

26:1-9 62,107
30:1-10 128,129
30:5f 55
30:9 129
31 89,118
Ezekiel
5:8f 93
11 31
22 31
36 31
37 31.37,48,55,
132,133,137
37:21 31
37:26 31
43 166
Daniel
9 108,133,181
9:24 109,133
9:26 62,107
9:26-27 106,108
9:27 108
12 59,74,123
12:1 129
12:1-2 125,127
12:1-3 129
12:7 59,127
12:9f 106
Hosea
1 118
2:1-2 40
2:15f 31
2:18f 31
2:18-23 40
3 40
5:15-6:3 30
8:1-10 62,107
8:8 29
10:15 62,107
13:13 123
13:14 70
Amos
3:3f 10
5:18f 11

9 118
Micah
1:2-4 178,179
3:9-12 178
3:12 62
4:1-4 178,179
Zechariah
11:6 62,107
9:14 34,131
14 179
Malachi
3:7 31
Matthew
8:10-11 144,146,
147,148
8:11-12 29,147,
149,150,151,
152,154.162
11:20-24 63
11:28f 43
12:41-42 62
12:43-45 117
12:49-50 12
16:27 19
16:27-28 49,119,
139
21:43 147
22 43
23 9,58
23:29f 55,79
23:31-36 6,7,64
23:34f 74
23:37 4,39,43
24 9,23,27,36,37,
58,120,122,129,
138,188
24:2 182
24:3 1,4,101,177
24:4-34 120
24:8 55,123
24:10-12 186
24:14 1,2,3,5,41,
44,59,89,103,

104,112,113,
164
24:15f 106
24:21 10
24:29f 140,141
24:29-31 55,132,
133
24:30 15,19,185
24:30-31 19,49,50
24:31 28,30,34,35,
36,39,58,131,
132,133,141
24:31-34 134
24:34 36,126,134
24:35 26
24:36-51 120
25 120
25:1-46 120
25:31f 11,39,49,
50,62,63,120
Mark
13 188
Luke
4 47
13:10-17 18
13:28f 155
13:33 7
14 43
16:16 52
18:1-8 186
19 150
21:6 182
21:20 61,107
21:20-24 11,106
21:22 51,60,66,67
21:22-28 105,106
21:28 109
21:28-32 92,119
23:44-45 81
John
3:13 152
5:28-29 67,68,127
11:47-53 132

17:4 76
18:38 80
19:4 80
19:6 80
19:30 75,76,80,81
Acts
  2:29f 153
  3:22f 12
  3:23f 24
  15 170,175
  15:1-2 164
  17 13
  24:14-15 68,71
  26:6f 71
  26:21-23 68,69,
      71,157
Romans
  2:28f 90
  7:7f 139
  8 19
  8:1-3 102
  8:17 79
  8:19 12
  8:23 69,71
  9 111
  9:1-4 69,71
  10 41,111
  10:14f 40
  10:20-21 21
  11 91,111,186
  11:25-27 33,91,97
  14:17f 170
1 Corinthians
  2:6f 89
  3:16 85
  5 77
  7-8 170
  10 170
  11:16f 78
  11:26 79
  15 68,70,127,139,
      144,146,147,
      148,149,150

15:19f 157
15:22 151
15:51 139
15:51-52 138
15:52 34,35,131
      132,138
15:54-55 70,71,74
15:55,56 146,151,
      157
2 Corinthians
  3 100,139
  3:7 100
  3:18 100
  5:1-3 111
  6:14-16 85
  6:16 32
  6:16f 42
Galatians
  3:10-13 139
  3:20-21 101,118
  4:22f 139
Ephesians
  1:7 97,99,101
  1:12-13 106
  1:12-14 98
  2:15 132
  2:17-22 132
  2:19f 85
  4:30 97,99,101,
      106
Philippians
  1:6 98
  2:5f 19
  3:1-5 90
  3:16-18 89
Colossians
  1 41
  1:18f 157,158,160
  2 84,167
  2:8 170,176
  2:11-13 40
  2:11-17 168
  2:14f 76,95,170,

      171,175
  2:16 171
  2:20-21 171
  3 176
  3:1f 19
1 Thessalonians
  4 141,142
  4:16 35,132
  4:16-17 140
2 Thessalonians
  1 13,19
  1:6f 13
  1:10 13,79
  2 141
Titus
  2:12f 41
Hebrews
  1 46
  2:5 46
  6:19f 153
  8 89
  8:1-2 85,91
  8:6-13 27
  9 97,99,104,153
  9:6-10 94
  9:8f 170
  9:23-24 85,86
  9:28 95
  10:1-3 94
  10:1-4 94
  10:5f 90
  10:37 99
  11 90,148,154
  11:35 154
  11:39-40 153
  12 148
  12:21f 90,148
1 Peter
  1:7 17
  2:6 17
  3:16 17
  5:1f 79

2 Peter
  3 21.23,171
  3:13 24,25
Revelation
  1:1-3 143
  1:5f 90
  3:9 13
  6:9f 143
  8-11 143
  10:6f 142
  11 154
  11:8 o
  11:15-19 142,143
  11:19 104
  15 154
  15:8 104
  11 109
  11:15f 110
  15 109
  16 109
  19:1-3 109,110
  21 21
  21:1f 40
  22:6f 26,143

Topical Index

A
Abomination of Desolation 36, 106,181
Abraham 12,14,29,96,97,144,146, 147,148,149,150,152,153,154, 155,157,162
Adoption 17,69
Ammillennialist(s) 91,120,121, 123,140,147,149

B
Babylon 4,26,31,109,137,154
Banquet 22,54,136,145,147,148, 149,150,151,152,154,155,157, 162
Beale, Greg 34,85,131
Blood 7,14,18,35,36,55,64,72,73, 74,78,80,87,94,98,99,109,110

C
Calvin, John 5,96
Chilton, David 13,14
Circumcision 40,84,90,168,170,
Circumcised 40,90,164,165,166, 168,175,
Covenant(s) 10,26,28,29,43,45, 50,60,69,72,101,104,108,109, 113,114,115,116,117,118,136, 146,147,151,152,153,166,167, 177,180,186
Covenant Eschatology 3,65
Covenant, New 10,22,26,27,31, 37,40,43,46,75,85,89,92,100, 109,113,118,119,180
Covenant, Old 2,3,6,10,13,15,20, 21,22,23,24,25,26,27,36,37,44, 46,50,51,60,65,70,72,76,84,85, 86,87,88,89,90,91,92,93,94,100, 101,103,104,110,111,113,118, 119,120,123,134,135,139,141, 142,143,146,147,151,152,153, 154,162,165,172,173,174,175, 177,180,181,186,188

Covenantal 10,14,26,30,39,60,61, 107,112,113,114,115,117

D
Death 19,25,45,46,49,50,53,55, 70,73,77,78,79,93,97,100,101, 102,104,114,119,133,136,139, 145,146,151,156,157,158,159, 160,161,163,169,174,175,184, 188
DeMar, Gary 132,133
Desolate 4,32,33,56
Destruction 1,5,6,9,10,11,12,13, 14,15,18,19,21,23,24,25,27,36, 52,53,55,57,59,60,65,72,74,84, 86,87,89,92,101,102,104,106, 108,109,110,111,112,113,116, 117,119,127,136,139,145,156, 164,172,173,174,175,176,177, 179,186,187,188
Dispensationalism 42,43,88,89, 90,123,169,176
Dispensationalist(s) 10,66,88,89, 91,106,107,

E
Element(s) 9,17,18,25,27,39,49, 58,149,171,172,175
Elliott, Mark 115
End of the age 1,4,5,6,23,24,28, 59,63,64,84,101,177,181,188
End of the world 115,120,187
End–time(s) 28,29,33,34,37,43, 45,48,50,123,127,177
End of Time 3,5,16,23,39,46,62, 96,97,120,127,138,147,155,156, 178,185
Eschatological 1,9,16,24,28,30, 31,32,35,37,39,45,47,50,51,52, 65,75,77,79,82,85,103,115,123, 124,131,143,153,177,181
Eusebius Pamphilius 177
Eusebius of Caesarea 118,177,

178,179

F

Frost, Sam 3,51,52,125,129,152, 155,169
Fulfilled 3,9,14,40,41,42,47,51, 52,54,57,59,60,61,62,64,65,66, 67,68,70,71,72,74,75,77,82,88, 93,105,107,120,123,125,127, 128,129,134,137,139,148,177, 179,180,181
Fulfillment 3,4,6,14,23,24,26,36, 37,40,41,45,47,50,51,52,57,60, 62,65,70,71,75,76,77,81,82,85, 91,92,107,108,134,139,148,150, 151,156,178,181,186
Futurism 11,156,157

G

Gathering 28,29,30,31,32,33,34, 35,36,37,39,40,42,43,44,45,47, 48,50,57,58,121,124,130,131, 132,135
Generation 1,7,8,36,37,41,45,46, 50,53,55,57,62,63,64,117,126, 134,139,173
Gentile(s) 21,22,28,41,48,63,69, 82,105,124,132,135,147,164, 165,167,168,169,170,171,172, 175,179,186,
Gentry, Kenneth 10,11,62,65,66, 67,68,70,71,72,74,115,116,120, 123,147
Glaser, Mitch and Zhava 34,131
Glorification 13,15,16,19
Glory 16,19,36,45,46,47,49,50,69, 79,86,92,97,100,105,106,110, 119,134
Gray, Timothy 186,188

H

Hagner, Donald 35,131,132
Harnack, Adolph 8
Heaven and Earth 24,26,27,178, 181,188
Hester, David 126,127,153,
Hollett, Brock 4

Hope(s) 3,4,24,32,39,44,48,68,69, 70,100,112,113,117,137,148, 149,150,154,156,176,178,183, 184

I

Ice, Thomas 11,61,62,106,107
Israel 5,9,10,11,12,13,14,18,22, 23,24,28,29,30,31,32,33,34,36, 37,38,39,40,41,42,43,45,47,48, 49,54,55,56,57,60,61,62,63,64, 65,69,70,72,74,76,77,80,84,86, 87,88,89,91,92.93,107,108,110, 111,113,115,116,123,124,128, 129,130,131,132,135,136,137, 141,142,144,146,147,151,152, 162,164,165,167,170,175,176, 177,184,186,
Israel Only 25

J

Jerusalem 1,2,4,6,7,8,9,10,11,14, 15,16,18,19,20,21,22,23,25,26, 27,28,31,32,33,34,36,37,38,40, 43,44,45,46,51,52,53,54,55,56, 57,58,59,60,61,63,64,65,66,68, 71,72,73,74,75,84,88,89,90,93, 101,102,103,104,105,106,107, 108,109,110,111,113,115,116, 117,118,119,120,125,130,132, 133,134,135,146,154,164,165, 166,169,170,171,172,174,175, 176,177,178,179,180,181,183, 184,185,188
Jews 7,8,12,13,14,21,31,63,93, 115,117,123,132,179,182,183, 184,185,188
Jordan, James 121
Judaizer(s) 40,164,165,166,167, 168,169,170,172
Judgment 4,9,10,11,13,14,17,18, 19,23,31,33,34,36,37,39,52,55, 57,58,59,60,61,62,63,64,65,74, 79,88,92,97,98,101,106,107, 108,109,110,118,119,120,124, 134,139,143,144,146,147,151,

152,154,173,178,181,185
Julian the Apostate 14,181,182,
183,184,185
Justin the Martyr 7,8
K
Kingdom 1,2,5,6,10,15,16,20,25,
27,28,29,30,32,37,39,41,42,43,
44,45,47,49,50,51,52,53,59,60,
65,75,77,84,88,89,90,91,92,93,
101,102,103,109,110,111,112,
113,117,118,119,120,124,129,
139,142,144,146,147,148,149,
150,151,152,155,162,164,165,
170,173,174,178,180,188
Kistemaker, Simon 160
Kline, Meredith 108,109,
L
Life 3,18,19,25,27,37,78,81,100,
101,102,112,114,115,118,119,
133,136,137,148,150,152,154,
156,157,158,159,161,162,168,
Luther, Martin 96,154
M
Martyr(s) 9,35,55,56,58,72,74,
143,152
Mathison, Keith 122
McDurmon, Joel 24,25,35,72,149
Messiah 12,14,19,22,27,30,31,37,
39,40,50,55,75,88,91,108,118,
119,124,129,164,165,173
Moses 12,14,57,60,68,69,70,75,
82,95,96,101,104,139,164,165,
169,170,175,180
Most Holy Place (MHP) 93,94,
95,96,97,99,100,101,104,105,
109,153,154
N
New Creation 2,20,21,22,23,24,
25,26,27,37,50,88,103,109,110,
111,112,119,120,125,168,181
Nolland, John 34,131
O
Olivet Discourse 1,11,14,27,28,
36,45,120,126,139,140,164

P
Parousia 1,19,70,104,141
Pitre, Brant 77,78,123
Postmillennialist(s) 91,120,123,
140,149
Preterist(s) 3,4,37,39,51,52,59,66,
72,125,152,169,176
Preterism 3,4,11,74
Promise(s) 3,9,13,14,22,23,25,31,
36,40,41,47,48,49,55,69,71,82,
91,92,115,130,135,136,150,153,
154,167,186
Promised 23,29,31,32,40,42,50,
92,115,134,137,154,164,175
Prophecy 3,14,20,21,22,23,24,33,
35,36,37,39,40,41,42,45,46,49,
51,52,57,58,59,64,65,66,67,71,
108,122,123,129,135,146,173,
179,181,182
Prophetic(ally) 39,44,53,143,144,
186
R
Redeem(ed) 38,40,41,43,44,56,
79,156
Redemption 40,41,42,47,49,69,
79,96,98,99,101,103,105,106,
107,109,
Regather(ed) (ing) 28,29,32,33,
36,48,131,135
Remnant 21,22,41,50,59,108,111,
124,135
Replacement 91
Restored 29,37,43,129,163
Restoration 28,31,33,36,37,42,43,
45,48,49,86,90,124,129,152,184
Resurrection 9,22,23,32,33,34,35,
36,37,39,40,42,43,44,48,52,54,
55,56,57,58,59,66,67,68,69,70,
71,72,73,74,75,82,96,97,100,
101,104,120,121,122,124,125,
126,127,128,130,131,132,134,
136,137,138,139,142,143,144,
146,147,148,149,150,151,152,
154,155,156,157,158,159,160,

195

161,162,168,169
Richardson, Joel 3,4
Riddlebarger, Kim 121,147
S
Sabbath(s) 169,29,76,84,166,167,
168,171,175,176
Salvation 11,21,22,28,33,34,38,
40,41,42,44,47,49,50,54,55,56,
57,59,61,65,78,82,88,91,92,93,
95,96,97,99,100,107,108,109,
110,111,122,145,146,153,164,
165,170,172,175,188
Schurer, Emil 122,123
Sproul, R.C. 176
Stevenson, Gregory 116,186
T
Tabernacle 32,85,91,94,111,187
Temple 4,5,6,7,10,13,14,15,20,27,
32,33,34,36,42,44,54,57,58,59,
64,73,77,80,81,84,85,86,87,88,
89,90,92,93,101,102,104,105,
109,112,113,115,116,117,118,
125,133,136,139,145,146,147,
164,165,166,167,172,173,174,
175,176,177,179,180,182,183,
184,185,186,187,188
Tribulation 10,11,13,18,19,36,55,
59,60,62,84,107,110,121,123,
124,125,126,127,128,129,134,
181
Trumpet 28,32,33,34,35,36,49,56,
57,58,121,130,131,132,133,134,
135,137,138,139,140,141,142,
143,
U
Uncircumcised 38,40,166
Uncircumcision 168
V
Vindication 9,11,13,14,15,16,18,
19,58
W
Watts, John 133
Welch, John 174
Wright, N.T. 18,48,170,171,

Z
Zion 38,40,42,43,45,46,47,49,54,
146,148,165,166
Zionism 176

Made in the USA
Coppell, TX
14 May 2024